D1566495

An Irishman in Dixie

AN IRISHMAN IN DIXIE

THOMAS CONOLLY'S DIARY
OF THE
FALL OF THE CONFEDERACY

EDITED BY
NELSON D. LANKFORD

UNIVERSITY OF SOUTH CAROLINA PRESS

Copyright © University of South Carolina 1988

Published in Columbia, South Carolina, by the
University of South Carolina Press

First Edition

Library of Congress Cataloging-in-Publication Data

Conolly, Thomas, 1823–1876.
　An Irishman in Dixie

　Bibliography: p.
　Includes index.
　1. Conolly, Thomas, 1823–1876—Diaries. 2. United
States—History—Civil War, 1861–1865—Personal
narratives. 3. Confederate States of America—History.
4. United States—Description and travel—1848–1865.
5. Irish—United States—Diaries. I. Lankford,
Nelson D. II. Title.

E605.C764　　　1988　　　973.7'82　　　88-1143
ISBN 0-87249-555-8

For J.A.L.

CONTENTS

ILLUSTRATIONS

PREFACE

Many books come into being through serendipity. So it was with this one, although the island in question was not Serendip but Korčula, off the Dalmatian coast of Yugoslavia. There by chance two guests at a wedding chose a topic of conversation that indirectly led to the publication of this book, but that is getting ahead of the story.

When Thomas Conolly returned home to Castletown House in 1865, he carried with him a diary containing his day-by-day observations of America at the close of the Civil War. What he did with this account is not known. Probably it was soon forgotten among the books and papers in his library. Conolly's descendants lived on at Castletown into the twentieth century, but in 1965 the house was sold out of the family. It stood empty for two years. In 1967 the founder-president of the Irish Georgian Society, the Hon. Desmond Guinness, purchased it in the nick of time in order to save it from ruin. The restoration effort began shortly thereafter under the guidance of the trustees of the Castletown Foundation, which now owns the house and administers it for the Irish Georgian Society. It was fortunate, indeed, that one of these trustees was Desmond Fitz-Gerald, the twenty-ninth Knight of Glin, of Glin Castle in County Limerick and an authority on Irish art, architecture, and furniture. For, having read widely about the proprietors of Castletown, he immediately recognized Conolly's diary when antique dealer Ronald McDonnell brought it to his attention. The diary is now one of the prized manuscripts on the Conollys owned by the Castletown Foundation.

The Knight of Glin therefore knew of the Conolly diary when, on a spring day in 1983, he visited the aforementioned island of Korčula. There the friends of Scottish brigadier Sir Fitzroy Maclean had gathered to celebrate the wedding of his son. Among the guests in addition to the Knight of Glin was an American, FitzGerald Bemiss, a trustee of the Virginia Historical Society. Thus, in a roundabout fashion, through the chance meeting of Irish and American guests at the wedding of a Scot on an island in Yugoslavia, a photocopy of the Civil War diary of Thomas Conolly was soon made available to the Virginia Historical Society by the Castletown Foundation.

I therefore would like to thank first of all the two trustees, the Knight of Glin and FitzGerald Bemiss, for their part in making this important source on the Civil War available to researchers in this country. I am especially indebted to two members of the staff at the Virginia Historical Society, Senior Librarian Howson W. Cole, for bringing the diary to my attention in early 1986, and Assistant Editor Sara B. Bearss for giving valuable advice on the transcription, annotation, and commentary. My other colleagues on the staff at the Society, especially Linda Leazer, Frances Pollard, Sarah Sartain, and Waverly K. Winfree, helped in many ways, and I thank them for their assistance. Jeff Nagel, whose woodworking skills are well known to his associates at the Society, revealed another talent in adapting a Civil War map for this book in order to illustrate Conolly's travels.

A portion of the diary, chapters 2 and 3, appeared in the January 1987 issue of the *Virginia Magazine of History and Biography*. The notes to those chapters are much improved, thanks to suggestions from readers of the *Magazine* who helped identify people Conolly mentioned only cryptically. Among those readers was John Warren Cooke, former speaker of the Virginia House of Delegates and son of the Major Giles Buckner Cooke who escorted Conolly around the defenses of Petersburg in 1865. Mr. Cooke brought his father's diary, which contains Major Cooke's comments on the M.P., to my attention and then graciously donated that important manuscript to the Virginia Historical Society.

Many others contributed in varying ways to the genesis of this book. Among those who gave special help and guidance were David F. Allmendinger, Jr., Christopher Calkins, John Warren Cooke, Lynda L. Crist, Gary W. Gallagher, James O. Hall, Robert K. Krick, George Nan, Richard J. Sommers, William A. Tidwell, Emory M. Thomas, John White, and Stephen R. Wise. I would also like to thank the staffs of Alderman Library, University of Virginia; Boatwright Library, University of Richmond; Irish Georgian Society, Castletown House, Ireland; National Archives, Washington, D.C.; Southern Historical Collection, University of North Carolina at Chapel Hill; Trinity College Library, University of Dublin; Virginia State Library.

Three individuals in Ireland, all trustees of the Castletown Foundation, aided my research in special ways. With characteristic generosity, Desmond Fitz-Gerald made his Dublin house available to me and my wife during our trip to Ireland in the summer of 1987. I shall always be grateful to him whenever I recall how pleasant it was to pore over Tom Conolly's papers in the comfort of the drawing room of 52 Waterloo Road. The Hon. Desmond Guinness too was a gracious host at his home, Leixlip Castle, where he showed me the London diaries of Tom Conolly, which he had discovered in a provincial antique shop. The third Castletown Trustee, Lena Boylan, has written widely on the history of Celbridge and the Conolly family and shared her knowledge cheerfully. She was the best-informed guide imaginable to show foreign visitors the home and local haunts of the master of Castletown.

At the University of South Carolina Press Warren Slesinger, the acquisitions editor, gave sustained and enthusiastic support.

My wife, Judy, read earlier drafts with a critical eye, unaffected by my year-and-a-half immersion into the life of Tom Conolly, and it is to her that I dedicate the book.

Many have helped save me from pitfalls, large and small, in preparing the diary for publication, but the responsibility for remaining errors of omission and commission is mine.

Tom Conolly will seem to some readers a wastrel of the first water, to others a charming and gracious eccentric. Whatever one's opinion on his personality, it should be agreed by all that students of the American Civil War have him to thank for visiting these shores when he did and for recording his observations at such length. Noting his popularity with tenants and gentry alike, and cognizant of his financial imprudence, the *Irish Times* perhaps got it right in its obituary notice on Conolly, calling him "genial, kindly, generous to a fault."

Nelson D. Lankford
Richmond, Virginia
August 1987

An Irishman in Dixie

INTRODUCTION

Late in February 1865, after the last southern port of any consequence had been closed to rebel shipping, one of the last friendly vessels to reach Confederate waters dropped anchor off the North Carolina coast and sent several passengers ashore. Among these travelers from the blockade runner *Owl* was the scion of one of the leading families in Ireland, a gregarious Tory backbencher and would-be entrepreneur in service to the southern cause, Mr. Thomas Conolly, member of the British Parliament and master of Castletown House in County Kildare.[1] An ardent partisan of the South, Conolly had decided on the voyage the previous autumn and, as he set out on this uncertain enterprise, began to keep a record of his experiences, the American volume of which is presented in this book.[2]

In brief, Conolly and a group of associates purchased and outfitted a steamship, the *Emily*, which they intended to sail to Wilmington, where they hoped to exchange the cargo at great profit for rebel cotton. Unfortunately for these merchant adventurers, the ship was damaged on the first leg of the voyage and had to turn back at Madeira. Conolly, however, pressed on as a passenger on another blockade runner in hopes that the *Emily* would follow after being repaired. He reached the South, met Jefferson Davis, dined with Robert E. Lee, saw Richmond fall, fled northward, and returned home to tell his tale. Although his diary tells an American story, the M.P. was clearly a stranger in the land he visited. It will help to explain the diary and its perspective, then, if something is said about Conolly's background before examining how and why this leading member of the Victorian gentry of Ireland chose to endure hardship and risk capture, injury, or worse.

---

[1]Lena Boylan, "The Conollys of Castletown," *Quarterly Bulletin of the Irish Georgian Society,* XI, no. 4 (1968), 44–45.

[2]See Appendix A for a description of his various records of the voyage.

3

Castletown House, Country Kildare, the first great Palladian country house in Ireland, built in the 1720s by Speaker Conolly on the River Liffey a dozen miles west of Dublin. *Castletown Foundation*

The story must begin with a civil war in Ireland, not America, and with the founder of the Conolly dynasty, not the diarist who presided over its decline. The founder, William Conolly (1662–1729), was the son of a humble inn-keeper in County Donegal, in the isolated far northwest of Ireland. Not content to follow in his father's footsteps, the publican's son kept an eye to the main chance, which for him came with the revolution the English called Glorious. As an ambitious Protestant lawyer noted for his drive and energy, he built the family fortune largely through shrewd dealings in confiscated estates after the battle of the Boyne in 1690. Thriving under the Protestant Ascendancy that dominated Irish life in the eighteenth century, he did so well for himself that he entered Parliament and became known forever after as Speaker Conolly for attaining that office in the Irish House of Commons. But he never forgot his modest origins or that he was Irish, not English. Further, he gloried in remaining a commoner and disdained the hereditary titles that would have been his for the asking.

The emblem of Speaker Conolly's success, and the family seat for over two centuries, was the magnificent house designed by Alessandro Galilei and

Thomas Conolly (1823–1876) sat in the House of Commons for County Donegal, the constituency of his father and of Speaker Conolly before him. This portrait was painted by William Osborne about five years after Conolly returned from his American travels. *Castletown Foundation*

built in the 1720s on the River Liffey a dozen miles west of Dublin. Castletown was the first great Palladian country house in Ireland, the largest private home in the nation, and a source of wonder and comment to the members of the Ascendancy elite who were entertained under its roof. It remains today what it was then, a classical testimony in fine Irish limestone to the social and cultural, as well as political, standing the family had attained in a single generation.[3]

[3]Maurice Craig, the Knight of Glin, and John Cornforth, "Castletown, Co. Kildare," reprinted from *Country Life*, CXLV (27 Mar., 3, 10 Apr. 1969); Desmond Guinness and William Ryan, *Irish Houses & Castles* (London, 1971), pp. 193–209.

Because Speaker Conolly had no children, Castletown and the vast network of landholdings that supported it passed to his nephew and then to his nephew's son, the first Thomas Conolly (1738–1803). This first Thomas and his wife, Lady Louisa Lennox, continued in extravagant style the Conolly presence in the leading circles of the Ascendancy. If, however, the eighteenth century began for the family with Speaker Conolly rising to prominence in the Dublin Parliament, it ended with Thomas giving warm support to the Act of Union, which, by joining England and Ireland, dissolved that same Parliament. By advocating union, according to one account, the first Thomas "surrendered his country, lost his own importance, died in comparative obscurity, and in his person ended the pedigree of one of the most respectable . . . families ever resident in Ireland."[4]

As the first Thomas Conolly and his wife had no children, the estate passed on the death of Lady Louisa in 1821 to Colonel Edward Michael Conolly, a great-great-great-nephew of Speaker Conolly and father of the Civil War diarist.[5] Despite the dissolution of the Irish House of Commons, the colonel, as proprietor of Castletown, did not neglect his civic duty under the new political dispensation. From 1832 until his death in 1848, he sat in the House of Commons at Westminster for a constituency in which he owned much property and to which his family could trace its humble origins—County Donegal.

By the time the colonel inherited Castletown, the family had long since ceased to be the simple folk that Speaker Conolly had liked to imagine they were. Furthermore, even before Colonel Conolly's day they had become more English than Irish. It is not surprising, then, that the second Thomas Conolly, the eldest of the colonel's ten children and the author of the diary presented in this volume, would think himself no different from other wealthy English country gentlemen whose estates happened to be in Ireland. He was educated at Harrow and Christ Church, Oxford, was a member of several London clubs, and in the British capital maintained a house on Hanover Square.

When he inherited Castletown in 1848 at the age of twenty-five, Thomas Conolly, known to all as Tom, became the object of the deference shown the owner of one of the largest and most lucrative estates in Ireland. As the

[4]Quoted in *DNB*, IV, 955. About this first Thomas Conolly the same source said, "he fancied he was a whig because he was not professedly a tory; bad as a statesman, worse as an orator, he was as a sportsman pre-eminent."

[5]Colonel Edward Michael Conolly (1786–1848), son of Admiral Sir Thomas Pakenham, married Catherine Jane Ponsonby-Barker in 1819 and changed his surname to Conolly upon inheriting Castletown (Burke's *Commoners* [London, 1836], II, 159–60).

eldest, Tom escaped the fates reserved to younger sons of gentry families, who typically were packed off to the army, the church, or the learned professions. Two of Tom's brothers, in fact, held army commissions. One was killed at Inkerman, and another won a Victoria Cross elsewhere in the Crimea.[6]

If the order of birth spared Tom Conolly from his brothers' need to find suitable occupations, in return it thrust upon him the many responsibilities attached to the role of master of Castletown. These were spread across the face of Ireland with the estates that had been handed down intact from the palmy, acquisitive days of Speaker Conolly. Besides Castletown, the family properties included Leixlip in County Kildare, Rathfarnham in Dublin, Ballyshannon and Parkhill in County Donegal, and lesser possessions in County Roscommon and the King's County.[7] Like his father before him, Tom held the leading posts of authority in the social structure of the counties in which he was a great landowner: justice of the peace and deputy lieutenant for both County Kildare and County Donegal and sheriff of the latter county as well.[8]

By the early Victorian period all was not well with the Conolly legacy, however. Mortgage encumbrances that had been piling up for years compelled Tom not long after his father died to sell large parts of the patrimony in order to satisfy the debts that he had inherited along with Castletown.[9] Nevertheless, the straightened circumstances in which he thus began his tenure as a legatee of Speaker Conolly did not stand in Tom's way. He quickly established a reputation for an extravagant style of living that surpassed even the eighteenth-century Thomas Conolly in profligacy. His pastime obsessions—in particular, riding to hounds in County Kildare and picking up prostitutes in London parks—Tom Conolly pursued with the energy expected of a young rake.[10]

Pastimes aside, with his estates Conolly also inherited commensurate political responsibilities. Landowners exercised great electoral influence, and, still possessing some of the largest holdings in Ireland, Conolly was

[6]Arthur Wellesley Conolly (1828–1854), captain, 30th Foot; John Augustus Conolly (1829–1889), lieutenant colonel, Coldstream Guards (Burke's *Landed Gentry* [1879], p. 355).

[7]Burke's *Commoners* (1836), II, 161. The King's County is now County Offaly.

[8]Ibid., p. 159; Edward Walford, *The County Families of the United Kingdom*... (London, 1864), p. 229.

[9]Boylan, "The Conollys of Castletown," p. 44.

[10]His other diaries provide ample evidence of both of these pastimes. He placed a mark, usually some form of "x" in his diary for each assignation with a lady of the evening. The "x" marks were especially plentiful during his attendance at the House of Commons. A representative entry from his 1857 diary gives the typical mixture of politics, sex, and remorse: "Up late & debauched—down to house *late* for Division. Dawdle the day thro! & "x" again evening. This sort of thing must come to an end."

expected to uphold the established agricultural interests. It would have been odd if he had not been chosen to succeed his father as Conservative M.P. for rural County Donegal, where the family had been held in awe, if not exactly in reverence, since the days of Speaker Conolly.[11] When he took his father's seat in the Commons, the population of Donegal was about a quarter of a million, and yet only several thousand men qualified to vote. In this political climate of limited franchise, social deference, and the open ballot, the wishes of the great landowners carried much weight with those of their tenant farmers who could vote.[12]

Although Tom Conolly never rose to ministerial rank at Westminster, unlike many of his fellows on the back benches he did actually speak on occasion in the House. And the voice with which he spoke was the expected one of landed privilege, cautioning against precipitate change, attentive to legislation of particular local interest, tenacious in support of the Protestant Ascendancy, and seemingly unaffected by the upheavals in Irish life that followed the Great Famine and depopulated the countryside. Strangely, although the parliamentary records reveal Conolly's opinions on salmon fisheries, his arguments on suspension of habeas corpus, and his thoughts on a host of other issues of greater or lesser import, they show him silent on the events that convulsed America in the early 1860s and eventually enticed him across the Atlantic.[13]

* * * *

If it could be said that British opinion was divided when the American Civil War began, it could be argued too that most Britons of Conolly's class favored the South, or at least viewed the conflict as the North's attempt to suppress a legitimate southern impulse for national self-determination. Many of them, like the Confederates they supported, focused on the idealism of a struggle for national independence and chose to ignore the iniquity of the South's peculiar institution and to deny that the system degraded the master

[11]His seat was contested only in the first of the three general elections—1852, 1857, and 1859—between his appointment and his voyage to America (*PERI*, pp. 83, 90, 95, 267).

[12]In 1831 County Donegal had a population of 298,104 and, in 1832, an electorate of 1,448. By 1861, after electoral reform and sharp decline in population, the ratio of electors to people had narrowed only from 1-in-206 to 1-in-51 (ibid., p. 267). On the influence of landlords, "at elections for the Counties of Donegal in 1852, Wicklow in 1857, and Dublin in 1865 it was, for example, the most Catholic areas which were the most Conservative—a sure sign of successful proprietorial activity" (K. Theodore Hoppen, *Elections, Politics, and Society in Ireland, 1832–1885* [Oxford, 1984], p. 163).

[13]*Hansard's Parliamentary Debates*, especially during the 1850s, contain enough lengthy accounts of comments Conolly made in the House to demonstrate that he took his parliamentary duties seriously.

as it oppressed the slave. It was thus a source of disappointment and frustration to Conolly and like-minded countrymen when the British government repeatedly spurned southern efforts to gain diplomatic recognition.[14] By fall 1864 all strategic initiative in the war had passed for good to the North. The serious reverses suffered by the Confederates that autumn—Sherman threatening Georgia, Grant investing Petersburg—pointed to the ultimate resolution of the conflict. If, however, these events quickened northern hopes for victory and progressively dismayed even optimistic southerners, in England the press continued to exaggerate rebel prospects for success. With, for example, the London *Times* belittling the significance of the fall of Atlanta, Conolly may be excused for thinking a voyage to the South still a reasonable risk in late 1864.

It is unclear how he came to be involved in an attempt to run the naval blockade that had been erected to strangle the foreign trade of the Confederacy.[15] Certainly, the increasing indebtedness he faced by 1864 enhanced the attractiveness of the investment. It is clear, however, that he did not initiate the enterprise of the *Emily*. Among his papers is a letter written to him just before the voyage from a cousin, Emily Barton, for whom the blockade runner may have been named.[16] "I am so glad to hear," she wrote, that "you will be one of us! & hope by this you have seen John Palliser as he is in Dublin just now[.] I have written to him by this post. Depend upon it 'The Emily' is destined to succeed and she is the most splendid blockading vessel that has ever left the Clyde—"[17] Other comments by Barton reinforce the impression that Conolly was brought into the affair late in the planning: "I may now mention a few of the shareholders names *in confidence*. Mr. Tottenham of Ballycurry Lord Charlemont Col Bushe, Sir B. Chapman Col McNamara and Lots of others whom you know. Please Let me have a line to say if you have seen Mr. Palliser & what you are going to do."[18]

Like the master of Castletown, John Palliser was a member of the close-knit Ascendancy gentry and, not surprisingly, a distant relative of both Conolly and Emily Barton. Palliser was more than just an Irish country

[14]See Donald Bellows, "A Study of British Conservative Reaction to the American Civil War," *Journal of Southern History*, LI (1985), 505–26; bibliographies in Frank J. Merli, *Great Britain and the Confederate Navy, 1861–1865* (1965; Bloomington and London, 1970) and Norman B. Ferris, *The Trent Affair: A Diplomatic Crisis* (Knoxville, 1977).

[15]See Stephen R. Wise, *Lifeline of the Confederacy; Blockade Running during the American Civil War* (Columbia, S.C., 1988).

[16]Emily Martha Barton, daughter of William Barton of Grove, County Tipperary, and Conolly's second cousin (Burke's *Landed Gentry* [1879], p. 86).

[17]Emily Barton to Thomas Conolly, 6 Nov. [1864], filed in Conolly's rough diary.

[18]Ibid.

squire, however. He was no stranger to North America and had led several surveying expeditions into western Canada before the war. What is more, he seems to have developed a reputation, albeit a minor and not especially successful one, in commercial ventures capitalizing on the American blockade.[19]

As early as July 1863, Palliser had begun negotiations to supply marine engines for the Confederate navy, a proposal that for unexplained reasons never got beyond the talking stage. In March 1864, however, he again came to the attention of southern officials when an agent in Liverpool sent Confederate Secretary of the Navy Stephen R. Mallory a proposal from Palliser to form a joint stock company of his "own immediate friends, each subscribing a few thousand pounds."[20] The goal of this venture was to "build a ship expressly for the purpose" of transporting the elusive marine engines. The Liverpool agent, Commander James D. Bulloch, was experienced in negotiating for desperately needed military supplies in Britain and was confident that Palliser's scheme would allow a ship to be built "without exciting any especial notice or comment here."[21] In fact, Palliser agreed that his consortium would build a ship designed according to the plans Bulloch had been refining for some months to suit his government's needs. As a result, Bulloch wrote his superior in Richmond that if the ship "ever reaches a Confederate States port, I venture to predict that you will not permit her to remain long in private hands." In the shadowy legal environment in which they operated, both parties, it would seem, were willing to take advantage of one another.

Mallory wrote Bulloch a month later saying that he had no interest in renewing the languishing discussion with Palliser about the marine engines—and said not a word about the grander scheme for shipbuilding. Nevertheless, it is likely that in the exchange between Palliser and Bulloch was born the idea that eventually launched the *Emily* and enticed Tom

[19]John Palliser (1807–1887), of Comragh House, near Kilmacthomas, Co. Waterford, led Canadian expeditions in 1847, 1857, 1858, and 1860 (*DNB*, XV, 117). The link among the three, Thomas Barton of Grove, was Palliser's and Conolly's great-uncle and Emily Barton's grandfather (Burke's *Landed Gentry* [1879], p. 86). In his log book for 8 December 1864 Conolly called Palliser "The author & founder of our Expedition."

[20]James D. Bulloch to S. R. Mallory, 19 Mar. 1864, *ORN*, ser. ii, II, 611–12. All quotations in this paragraph are from this letter.

[21]James D. Bulloch (1823–1901) wrote *The Secret Service of the Confederate States in Europe* . . . (2 vols; reprint ed.; New York and London, 1959). See also Warren F. Spencer, *The Confederate Navy in Europe* (University, Ala., 1983), pp. 193–96; Wise, *Lifeline*, chap. 2.

Conolly to leave the comforts of Castletown for adventure across the water.[22]

Even though Conolly was not the driving force behind the voyage of the *Emily,* once he became a party to the plans his prominence gave the enterprise a new character. Further, despite Emily Barton's secretive tone, Conolly's involvement became widely known almost at the outset—for notice of it soon appeared in the press. The Liverpool *Albion* was the first to carry the story.

> A rumour difficult to credit, but from the manner in which it is put forward, still harder to refute, has reached us, to the effect that an M P, of large fortune and commensurate eccentricity, is about to seek a new excitement in "running the blockade." The motive impulse is, of course, sympathy with the Southern cause; but it would seem that although of acres broad, he is not entirely blind to the commercial advantages of the operation. . . . He will be only in a position to fulfil the expectations which he has created if he succeeds in getting through, and that contingency must have been rendered vastly more difficult of fulfilment by the open manner in which his preparations have been talked about. Need it be added that the gallant, adventurous, loquacious M P is a native of the sister isle?[23]

If the report is to be credited—and, in its favor, its reference to Conolly's garrulous nature was borne out in the comments of those whom he later met in America—the M.P. himself may have been the cause for the disclosure.

* * * *

On 26 November 1864 Tom Conolly set out from the country home of a kinsman, Lord Langford, to a rendezvous in south Wales with the *Emily.*[24] The vessel had just left the bustling Clyde shipyards, which had prospered greatly from the schemes and ambitions of blockade-running entrepreneurs. A paddle-wheel steamer of about 220 feet in length, the *Emily* presented a sharp appearance and, it was said, could make 20 knots in fair weather.

[22]S. R. Mallory to James D. Bulloch, 19 Apr. 1864, *ORN,* ser. ii, II, 628. In Conolly's log book is a document dated July 1864 that sets out the costs of the *Emily* and the expected revenues from one voyage to "Confederacy and Back," purporting to show a net profit of £6,500 on an investment of £41,000. Probably antedating the M.P.'s involvement, the document most likely was drawn up by one of the earlier partners and a copy found its way into Conolly's hands in the autumn.

[23]Liverpool *Albion,* 12 Dec. 1864; in Conolly's log book is a clipping of the same article as reprinted in another, unidentified newspaper.

[24]Conolly's rough diary begins on 26 November 1864 as he left Lord Langford, his nephew, who lived at Summerhill, a grand Palladian house in County Meath that burned during the Troubles in 1921.

Although just built, her white-painted smokestacks were already stained red with rust by the time she arrived at Cardiff to take on cargo, some of which no doubt went below the false bottom she was said to have. With luck, on the return voyage the *Emily* could accommodate a thousand bales of southern cotton.[25]

After a week during which last-minute snags multiplied and "warnings of all sorts were volunteered by officious friends," the ship left Great Britain on the seventh of December with its cargo and with Conolly and three other partners in the venture.[26] Only those four chose to monitor the fortunes of their investment at first hand. The others more prudently awaited word of the outcome from the security of their Mayfair townhouses or their snug hearthsides deep in rural England and Ireland.

In the earliest comments he wrote down on board ship, Conolly revealed something of his motivations for joining the enterprise. He felt an "Intense Desire of adventure & this one particularly, hallowed as it is by the great Cause of the South," because much of his life "had been wasted in inaction or what strongly resembled it going round a profitless & uninteresting routine."[27] Even more to the point, he envied "the Honorable Paths of Enterprize open to all younger sons and fortunate heirs of their own brains" and chafed at the responsibilities of being master of Castletown, "the weight of so call'd & often-times miscalled Property[;] mere Property shackles of subservience to countless others."[28] Although the voyage was intended to bolster his anemic finances, there is no reason to doubt that he also viewed the adventure of blockade-running as a chance for temporary escape from the bonds of tradition and custom that he felt were stifling him. Having made his decision, he could then disdain those people "born with a quiet, contented, mole-like disposition & sleek exterior whose only wish is to be passive enjoyers of the good things" and who were content "as long as their belly is full & their bottom warm."[29] Ironically, his detractors would use much the same language to describe Conolly.

No sooner did the *Emily* enter the Bristol Channel than the sky lowered and a gale arose and lashed the steamer for most of the eight-day passage to Madeira. Although Conolly avoided the seasickness that bedeviled his associates, he did not escape the rolling and pitching of the ship. Once he was thrown across the galley, came down on a saucepan of soup just taken off the

---

[25]U.S. consul, Cardiff, 8 Dec. 1864, T375, NA; document in log book describing the *Emily*.
[26]Rough diary, 5 Dec. 1864.
[27]Ibid., 6 Dec. 1864.
[28]Ibid.
[29]Initial entry in log book, Dec. 1864.

fire, and, in trying to break his fall, brought down a bin of condiments, dumping treacly molasses all over his clothes and curry powder on his hair.[30] As the storm abated shortly before landfall, he could happily turn his thoughts to the opportunity to "re-visit my old haunts" at Funchal. Among the people he met there were numerous other traveling Britons, including some of his vast cousinage, and islanders of his acquaintance from an earlier visit to Madeira.

Hanging over the expedition, however, was the knowledge that the *Emily* had sustained crippling damage during the storm. Accordingly, Conolly and his companions had to submit to the findings of a naval board of inquiry that would decide the fate of their ship. Five days before Christmas the board, which including the *Emily's* captain, concluded that the steamer was too severely damaged to proceed across the Atlantic without repair.[31] The finding came as no surprise to the four partners, and they accepted the verdict without complaint. At first Conolly was inclined to stay at Funchal and prolong his socializing while the ship was refitted. When the opportunity arose, however, he and Colonel William Bushe decided to cut short their merrymaking and proceed as ordinary passengers aboard another ship to Bermuda and, with luck, to Wilmington.[32] There they would await the arrival of the *Emily,* which, in the meantime, would be taken by the two commercially more experienced partners, John Palliser and Robert McDowell, to Cadiz for repairs.[33]

Conolly bore the ill fortune lightly. He took comfort in securing, within three days of the inquest, a berth on the *Florence,* bound for Bermuda. Then, when he determined that that blockade runner would not sail until early in the new year, he immediately set in train plans for a grand entertainment for the English and Portuguese society of Funchal. With his inclination for the melodramatic, he styled the affair the "Ball of the Buccaneers."[34]

---

[30]Log book, 12 Dec. 1864.

[31]"Report of Survey," signed and dated 20 Dec. 1864, in log book. Conolly wrote, "this is a serious day in the History of the Emily . . . which we had hitherto more or less shunned." The American consul, an Englishman, "treated us with the greatest of kindness tho' much criticized by his wife as buccanneers."

[32]William Daxon Bushe, former lieutenant colonel, 7th Hussars, in India.

[33]British merchant Robert McDowell, late of New Orleans, had prior involvement in the blockade-running business and was Palliser's original partner in the shipbuilding scheme proposed to Bulloch in March 1864 (*ORN,* ser. i, XVII, 280, ser. ii, II, 611–12). While at Madeira, Conolly noted that another blockade runner, also named *Emily,* arrived in port. Somewhat larger than Conolly's *Emily,* this ship, to confuse matters further, had left the Clyde estuary on the same day as the smaller vessel.

[34]Log book, 28 Dec. 1864.

Blockade runners at anchor. Conolly included this photograph among his mementoes of his American voyage and labeled it "The Little Emily," indicating that one of the ships seen here was the one he and his partners had purchased to run the blockade. *Castletown Foundation*

Perhaps he would have been less frivolous had he known that other parties besides the "officious friends" who implored him not to sail had taken an interest in the *Emily* even before he set eyes on her at Cardiff. For whatever reason—perhaps her distinctive, rakish lines, or perhaps some more damning evidence—the *Emily* had struck William Cook, United States vice consul at Glasgow, as a blockade runner, and he sent a message to the State Department the day before she left the Clyde estuary for Wales. The consul at Cardiff also wrote the department of his suspicions about the *Emily* shortly after she cleared the Welsh harbor. Thomas H. Dudley, United States consul in Liverpool, had additional news for his government about the venture. He

Captain John Newland Maffitt (1819–1886), "the prince of the privateers," brought Conolly to America on the last voyage of the CSS *Owl* to the North Carolina coast. *Virginia Historical Society*

had been intrigued by the article in the Liverpool *Albion* announcing that a wealthy M.P. was about to run the blockade and sent a copy to Washington two days after the notice appeared. These dispatches from Glasgow, Cardiff, and Liverpool were on Secretary of State William Henry Seward's desk early in the new year and, as it turned out, well before Conolly reached America. In December the Federal government had not as yet connected Conolly with the *Emily* or with the unnamed parliamentarian in the newspaper account. That state of ignorance, however, would not last.[35]

[35]U.S. consul, Glasgow, 18 Nov. 1864, T207, U.S. consul, Cardiff, 8 Dec. 1864, T375, U.S. consul, Liverpool, 14 Dec. 1864, T141, NA.

Bidding farewell to Madeira, Conolly and Bushe sailed west on the *Florence* for nine days and reached St. George's Harbor, Bermuda, on 13 January.[36] This notorious haven for blockade runners impressed Conolly as a "robbers den" of pubs, brothels, and all manner of shady characters: "Hogarth ought to have seen this place & is the only one who could portray it."[37] If the artist had done so, and had access to the M.P.'s Bermuda diary, he would not have placed Conolly entirely on the sidelines of the debauchery. On the very first evening in port, Conolly wrote of "prowling" about the harbor, picking up women, and concluded, "See another specimen 'Jane Young' very fine woman—but rather given up to the Blockade Bravos."[38]

After observing, and participating, for twelve days in the sailors' revelry, Conolly and Bushe continued with the *Florence* to the Bahamas. At Nassau they quickly made contact with business friends of Palliser and McDowell, dined with Confederate officers, and met all of the important civil and military officials in that diminutive outpost of the empire. Indeed, the governor invited the M.P. to the opening of the colonial assembly, at which Conolly heard him, as suited a proper Victorian administrator, give "a fiery speech cheifly about yellow fever & sewers."[39]

Conolly left Nassau in the *Florence* on the second of February, apparently trying to run the blockade, but a collision at sea with another vessel forced the ship to return to port on the fifth. The M.P. did not leave the islands again until the end of the month.[40]

* * * *

Before letting Conolly tell his own story of his three months in America, some words on the state of the war are in order. From the first of his scrib-

[36]The local newspaper listed prominent passengers on the ships that entered and cleared customs at St. George's, but Conolly's name did not appear in the lists for the *Florence* (*Bermuda Royal Gazette*, 17, 31 Jan. 1865).

[37]Thomas Conolly to Harriet Conolly, 19 Jan. 1865, retained copy filed in rough diary.

[38]Log book, 13 Jan. 1865.

[39]Rough diary, 1 Feb. 1865. Rawson William Rawson (1812–1899) had served in Canada, Mauritius, and southern Africa before appointment in 1864 as governor of the Bahamas (*Who Was Who... 1897–1916* [London, 1920]). The press account listing the guests to this event included "Conolly, Mr. (M.P. for Donegal) and Mrs. Conolly"—until 1868 there was no Mrs. Conolly (*Nassau Guardian*, 8 Feb. 1865).

[40]In his rough diary Conolly entered only dates, without explanation, for the abortive voyage. The *Richmond Whig* of 9 March 1865 carried a notice from Nassau dated 16 February: "The Hon. Mr. Connolly, member of Parliament from Ireland ... was on the Florence. She collided in the night with a bark, carrying away her wheel, &c. The bark was not seriously injured and no lives were lost. The Florence put back to Nassau and the member of Parliament is still enjoying himself in this quarter of her Majesty's dominions."

blings on the voyage, it is clear that Conolly took an overly optimistic view of the Confederacy's hopes. At Funchal on Christmas Day, for example, he wrote on hearing news of the war of "Sherman still uncaptured near Savannah."[41] Such a perception was not in the circumstances as naive as hindsight makes it seem. Given the skewed reporting of the prosouthern British press, it is not hard to see how Conolly was misled into thinking the South still possessed the might and the will yet to seize its independence. If Conolly was ignorant of military events and the British press deluded in its perspective, however, the hard captains in whose ships the M.P. traveled were not so sanguine and knew that the war, and the blockade-running business with it, was winding down. Indeed, the reason why so many blockade runners were riding at anchor at St. George's Harbor when Conolly arrived was that they were quickly running out of destinations still in Confederate hands. Also during Conolly's time at Bermuda the news came that Fort Fisher, which guarded the entrance to the last important rebel port, Wilmington, had fallen. Thus, when the M.P. learned later in Nassau that Captain John Newland Maffitt was willing to take him to the North Carolina coast on the blockade runner CSS *Owl*, even he should have realized that this would be his last opportunity to slip past the U.S. Navy and see the shriveling Confederacy.[42]

By this time Maffitt, known as the "prince of the privateers" to admirers and a piratical turncoat to northerners, was one of the last authentic rebel heroes still on the high seas. His charting of southern waters for the U.S. Navy before the war proved an ideal apprenticeship for his Confederate career, first as captain of the commerce raider CSS *Florida* and later as successful commander of blockade runners. Indeed, it had been Maffitt who, on his last run to Wilmington, had narrowly escaped capture and returned to Bermuda with the news that Fort Fisher had fallen and with it access to the last important port. Conolly crossed paths with Maffitt at Nassau, where the captain was waiting for further developments to help him decide his course. He chose at length to sail to Havana, where he hoped to collect the last of the blockade runners and attempt a final voyage to Galveston, Texas. Isolated from the principal theater of the war, the trans-Mississippi Confederacy was not an ideal destination, but Maffitt was unwilling to end his blockade-running career with his hands at the wheel of a fully loaded ship, and a very fast one at that. Before turning the *Owl* south to Cuba, however, he made one last trip to the North Carolina coast to drop

[41]Log book, 25 Dec. 1864.
[42]For John Newland Maffitt (1819–1886), see *DAB*, XII, 195–96; Emma Martin Maffitt, *The Life and Services of John Newland Maffitt* (New York and Washington, D.C., 1906).

off Conolly, two other passengers, and, it was rumored, important dispatches for Richmond.

By the time he left Nassau, then, Conolly must have known that the *Emily*
would not be repaired in time to run the blockade. Her cargo, divided "in
pretty nearly equal proportions with articles of comfort for the soldiers and
articles of luxury for the ladies," if the British press could be believed, and
including saddles for General Lee and his staff, according to an officer who
saw much of Conolly in Virginia, would never be of assistance to the Confederacy.[43] Still, Conolly's impulse for adventure was intact and his desire to
visit the South undimmed.

Because he succeeded, he must have been one of the very last foreigners
to arrive in rebel territory.[44] With the major Confederate ports in hostile
hands, it no longer mattered that the blockade had often been only a nuisance to the likes of Captain Maffitt—if there were no ports, there would be
no easy way for foreign visitors to see what was left of the Confederacy.
Beset from all quarters by invading armies, the area under the control of the
Richmond government had withered considerably by the winter of 1864–
65. More alarming to the Confederates was the growing fear that there was
nothing they could do to retard the progress of their enemies. There cannot,
then, have been many foreigners who reached the citadel of the dying cause
in the last months before its fall. As a well-connected member of the British
Parliament, Conolly was able to meet any southern leader he wished, and
this access put him in a position to observe daily life among the Richmond
elite. He did not neglect to comment, however, on conversations with lesser
officials, private soldiers, and even servants.

The value of his diary does not lie in any perceptive analyses, certainly. His
observations were often naive, as when he blithely expressed faith in ultimate Confederate victory while all around him the southern armies were
melting away, and his appetite for dinner parties and picnic tours of the front
lines admitted little room for introspection. Perhaps it is just as well that
Conolly was not a refined man of letters but a somewhat eccentric and
superficial sporting country gentleman given to assiduous notetaking. A

[43]Liverpool *Albion*, 12 Dec. 1864. According to Maj. Gen. Cadmus Marcellus Wilcox, who
accompanied Conolly from Raleigh, N.C., to Richmond, Va., "On board the Owl was a full set of
horse equipments, saddle, bridle, &c., for Gen. Lee and each member of his staff, presents from
Mr. Conley. They were never received" (*SHSP*, IV, 22n). Writing twelve years after the fact, Wilcox may have confused the *Owl* with the *Emily*. It is unclear whether Conolly transferred more
than his personal baggage from the *Emily* to the *Florence* to the *Owl*. When he separated from
the *Emily* at Madeira, he still hoped the ship would reach the South.

[44]See Ella Lonn, *Foreigners in the Confederacy* (Chapel Hill, 1940), pp. 358–59. Although
she calls the M.P. "Peter Connolly," she says he was the very last foreign visitor.

more serious pro-Confederate diarist might have ruminated more in abstractions about the collapse of "southern civilization" and noted fewer details than appear in Conolly's vivid descriptions of people and places in those last hectic days—descriptions that give us insight into the momentous events to which Conolly was witness even if he did not fully comprehend them himself.

The diary opens with an account of his last days in the Bahamas as Conolly prepared to turn his attention from "all the faire dames of Nassau" to final preparations for sailing with Maffitt and the *Owl* to the North Carolina coast.

CHAPTER ONE

"FROM NASSAU TO DIXIE"

THURSDAY, 23 FEBRUARY[1]

Tuesday was Mrs. Harris' balle at wh we met all the faire dames of Nassau. Mrs. Rawson[2] the Governors wife was kind enough to ask us to a ball on that day week, but no The fates had arranged us for Dixie & quiet communications had taken place with Capt Maffitt, Heiliger[3] & B. B.[4] & all was in train— So next day by 9 30 I went aboard the Owl & seeing Heiliger & Maffitt together explained my wishes & meeting with a favourable reception I immediately proceeded with Bogert[5] to comply with the Customs Ho reg. & then aboard Florence[6] & finding Capt De Forest at Dinner join them & explain my business, after C. Owens tells me to come early next day with

[1]The first entry begins on the back of the title page and carries a marginal heading, "Log of the Owl Capt. Maffitt C.S.N. from Nassau to Dixie." This first entry was apparently written on board the *Owl* on 24 February and included events of the three preceding days. The *Nassau Guardian* of 25 February confirmed the *Owl's* departure on 23 February.

[2]Mary Anna Sophia Ward had married Governor Rawson in 1850 (*Who Was Who . . . 1897– 1916* [London, 1920]).

[3]Louis Heyliger, Confederate commercial agent in the Bahamas throughout the war. He knew Conolly's associate, Robert McDowell (*ORN*, ser. i, XVII, 280). See also Wise, *Lifeline*, chap. 2.

[4]Conolly's partner, Lt. Col. William Daxon Bushe.

[5]Probably the G. C. Bogert whose advertisement appeared in the 28 April 1864 issue of the London *Index*, a pro-Confederate newspaper published by the "Southern Independence Association": "Bogert & Co. Auctioneers and Commission Merchants, Nassau, N.P. Consignments Solicited. G. C. Bogert, Late of New Orleans, La." Bogert, like Heyliger, was a friend of Conolly's associate, Robert McDowell.

[6]Cargo manifest for Conolly's ship from Madeira to Bermuda: "*Florence*, about 490 tons, St. George's [Bermuda] for Nassau, January 24, 1865, Samuel De Forest, master: Per entry: 504 bags coffee, 600 barrels pork." The *Owl* left Bermuda for Nassau two days later (Frank E. Vandiver, ed., *Confederate Blockade Running Through Bermuda, 1861–1865: Letters and Cargo Manifests* [Austin, 1947], p. 146).

20

Lighter Dine at the 1.W.I.[7] Mess with large party McAllister, B B, Phillips[8] &c up at 8 & down to get lighter & remove goods from Florence to Owl, Considerable difficulty owing to the way they were stored under the Coffees— nearly stifled in the hold with a gang of black fellows moving the bags of Coffee & then with much labor getting out my cases. Aboard Owl by 2 all safe— up to Hotel & Bogerts money £50 & pay bill meet Lou McAllister & Maggie Smith & walk them up to my house—dear little Lou, Oh dont go away Mr Conolly—Dinncr &—good bye to all my friends dear old Phillips & George accompany me on board & see me fairly dressed in my sea clothes, my red breeches & sea boots—The Carpenters still at work at the whale-back for the steerage. Maffitt comes aboard at 5.30 & immediately knocks off the carpenters the work not half done & prepares to start without a Pilot Dont get under weigh till 7. & then a series of disasters which wd have scared a man of different metal from Maffitt who succeeded by 8 in getting to sea, setting his course & then wiping the anxious sweat off his brow gave us our quarters with seamanlike cordiality & cocktails all around told us we must put up with 'rough & tumble' but he hoped to land us all safe in Dixie—

After a long suspense the daylight gradually declining & the lights of Nassau beginning to show in the darkness the order to stand by to test her [cable?] & then the wheels began to turn & we moved off, B. B & I looking over the Port Quarter. By Jove he shaved that vessel very close & then By Jove look ye here & crash & brush close to another with some damage. Port hard a port and back her steam roaring and fretting and [*illegible*], but before we could well back her or stop her way were in close contact with another barque & broke her bowsprit. The vessel being a good deal slewed out of her course then the backing began & before you could say crack a regular crash on the side of H.M.S. "Lily"[9] showed how dangerous was our position, However Maffits clear voice was heard "full speed" & altho we were so far slewed round that she could not make the passage out he brought her right round & determined on backing her out, wh after some suspense & a good deal of difficulty the wheel becoming for a short time engaged, we affected—

This whole business gave me a great idea of Maffitts coolness & capacity for all our difficulty arose from the 1st collision & the necessity of changing the straight course wh. followed from that, but considering the darkness, the

---

[7]The First West Indian Regiment.

[8]In his log book Conolly called Phillips "the barrack master & store keeper who has the nicest & best situated house in Nassau."

[9]HMS *Lily*, commanded by Algernon C. F. Heneage, whom Conolly met there, had arrived in Nassau on 4 February (*Nassau Guardian*, 8 Feb. 1865).

narrow & dangerous entrance to the harbour & the 3 partial collisions it was plucky! to go out backwards, being the only way he could manage it Thus[10]

This entrance even in day is very dangerous being both narrow & turning & has been the scene of many calamities 2 wrecks[11] one on either side witnessing the Fact—

Shortly after we all turned in Sterrett[12] B. B & I in the wheel house on the Bridge. The Capt. having given us possession of it. & very good quarters, we lay down just as we were & found the sun shining at 7. on Friday 24th Feb.

FRIDAY, 24 FEBRUARY

Up immediately beautiful weather steamed all day at 11 Knots all going right read "Pearl of Pearl River," a story of slavery & whittle a large club of Madeirawood left by the Carpenters at the Whaleback house sighted vessell a brig bound out spent evening in Capt Maffitts room his opinion of the Irish & his idea of treating them "Give Paddy once an idea of your Justice & then you may treat him as unjustly as you please"[13] Story of his receptions when commanding Florida[14] & in Ireland Discuss Genl Lee[15] Mrs. De Rosset[16] & & &—cocktails. Bed The wheel house is occupied for steering as the after wheel is damaged & so we are obliged to make a bed of straw on deck & sleep very well notwithstanding the rain—

SATURDAY, 25 FEBRUARY[17]

up at 5 before sunrise—Cocktails Fine sunrise 1/4 7—

Fine weather rolling sea the Gulph Stream bright green water Bk & dinner good!

[10]At this point Conolly drew a diagram of the zig-zag course Maffitt followed to back out of the harbor.

[11]Footnote: "Wreck of the Agnes Louise on the port & the S. Nereid on the starboard reef."

[12]Footnote: "danced with Mrs. Sterrett at Col. Maffitts 2nd Ball." See entries for 8 and 22 March. Identified by signature at back of the diary as "W. B. Sterrett Saint Louis Missouri," he was heavily involved in blockade running (*OR*, ser. iv, III, 156–57).

[13]Although born, appropriately, at sea, Maffitt himself came from a Protestant Irish family.

[14]The CSS *Florida*, a highly successful commerce raider under Maffitt's command during 1862–63 (*ECW*, p. 264).

[15]Presumably Gen. Robert Edward Lee (1807–1870), whom Conolly would meet later. See entries for 16, 30 March.

[16]Mrs. Louis H. DeRosset, wife of a Confederate official in Nassau (James Sprunt, *Chronicles of the Cape Fear River*... [Raleigh, 1914], pp. 425–27). Conolly met her on board the *Florence*.

[17]Marginal note: *"My birthday 42."*

Young Anderson[18] the 3rd officer very hands. fellow he was with Semmes[19] in "the Alabama"[20] when she engaged the Kearsarge & went down & was picked up by the Deerhound

Gave him a picture of Mrs. de Rosset another to Capt. Maffitt

Smoke & read—

SUNDAY, 26 FEBRUARY

Very cold night & no covering got me up by 4. & find we had made 8 fathoms sounding & were standing on & off waiting for light to make our destination at daylight saw the loom of the land thro' thick mist tho' it was 9 o'clock before we could see it distinctly & then it was only 100 yds distant from us, a very low coast covered with brush we hugged the shore till 10.30 when we cast anchor opposite to Shallotte bar.[21]

Shallotte inlet wh could not be entered except at high water. I immediately asked the Captain to put B. B self & Mr. Sterrett on shore immediately He consented & lowered a boat at once into which We got the sea running high when Pilot shoved off without B. B. who was as usual late—So away we go & soon saw the bar of the river foaming & roaring, with breakers all across we were soon among them & after passing one or two rollers with a very unpleasant heave a third & larger one broke over our boat swamping her & pitching us all over into the surf we soon righted the boat & succeeded in capturing the floating luggage & throwing them into the boat still half full of water when we shoved her on through the surf till we got to a tongue of Land & carried out our things then dragged the boat across a long neck of sand right into the Shallotte River—We then pulled up the river to the village of same name & there pulling our boat up on the shore[22] & getting out our baggage & stowing it all under a deserted boat which we turned over to make a roof for it as it had not ceased raining since we left the ship & we were doubly drenched with salt & rain water we then started with McKensie the Pilot who had belonged to Shallotte before the war[23] & soon came upon

[18]Eugene Anderson Maffitt (d.1886), eldest son of Captain Maffitt (Maffitt, *Maffitt*, p. 344).

[19]Raphael Semmes (1809–1877), admiral, C.S.N. (*BDC*, p. 380).

[20]The commerce raider CSS *Alabama* was sunk by the USS *Kearsarge* in 1864 off the coast of France. Many of the crew were rescued by the British ship *Deerhound* (*ECW*, pp. 3–4).

[21]Shallotte, North Carolina, near the South Carolina border about 35 miles southwest of Wilmington and several miles inland from the point at which Conolly came ashore.

[22]Footnote: "find relicks of the Yank in the shape of 3 hundred pound Parrot shells on the beach aha!"

[23]Marginal note: "Fair bluff Fayetteville."

Painted at the back of Conolly's diary, this watercolor of coming ashore at Shallotte Inlet, North Carolina, is labeled "My Arrival in Dixie." The _Owl_ is visible at the right. _Castletown Foundation_

some deserted houses, evidences of late Yankee raids & after a walk of a mile thro woods & swamp found one of comfortable appearance with the hospitable smoke curling from the chimney This lookd better & McKensie entered & succeeded being known to Mrs Pigott the inmate in calming her apprehension that the Yanks were Come again They had taken all her pigs & poultry on the previous Wed. so we moved off by McKensies instructions to seek shelter higher up & about 2 miles further found a nice family of same name also known to McKensie The women were all in the house & were much scared at our approach but were quickly reassured—! and then sent off for Mr Pigott "Massa John" to give information & assistance. We then learnt that Wilmington[24] whither we had purposed to go had fallen on the previous Tuesday & several of the neighbors of the village killed & Captured on that occasion that other Strong places Augusta, Columbia[25] & several other places were in their hands—We wrote this to Capt Maffit & asked him

[24]Footnote: "37 miles distant from Shallotte. See Illustrations in Appx." Although he had known that the forts guarding the entrance to the Cape Fear River, which led to Wilmington, were in Federal hands, Maffitt did not know if the town itself had fallen. He must have expected that his passengers would not have great difficulty reaching Wilmington from Shallotte.

[25]Columbia, South Carolina, had fallen on 17 February.

Conolly labeled this watercolor, which he painted at the back of his diary, "Weary Pilgrims of the Swamps of N.C." On the horse is "Massa John" Pigott pulling the baggage cart, followed by W. S. Sterrett, Conolly, and William Allen Selden, Jr. *Castletown Foundation*

to send us rifles as we must now walk & defend ourselves on the way & having got a good dinner go down & wait for B. B whom we expect to return with the Pilot—Darkness comes & no boat so order a nigger Henry to be on the shore at daylight to report & make ourselves very snug with 2 charming hostesses Mrs & Miss Pigott & two beautiful little boys Jimmy & Wesley— They make a roary fire & after an excellent supper of broiled ham & coffee with their bully sweet potatoes & some ground peas we got out all our things that had been drenched & hung them round the fire & laid our plans for the morrow. Mr Pigott (Massa John) volunteered to guide us thro the Forest 25 miles to [*illegible*] ferry on the Wackawmaw river[26] he taking our baggage with his neat little horse We are then to get the best information of the Yankees & march for Whitesville or Fair bluff[27] so as to get beyond their lines & eventually 170 miles make some railway not cut off wh shall take us

[26]The Waccamaw River, flowing roughly parallel to the coast from North Carolina into South Carolina, ran across Conolly's line of march about 12 miles inland from Shallotte.

[27]Villages in Columbus County, North Carolina. Whiteville was about 30 miles from Shallotte.

to Richmond 2 pipes of Tobacco & then to bed, I occupy 1 bed with Mr Sterrett & young Selden[28] Sleep with Massa John on the floor of the same room
the door-way of wh is hung over with a gauze curtain thro' wh we can see
the jovial blaze in the large room—

MONDAY, 27 FEBRUARY

Up at 5.30 after a splendid sleep. Go out to look after our comrades &
before I can get to the landing place in the creek meet the nigger Henry who
tells us that the Steamer is gone & no boat So B.B & the rest are back to Nassau So much for his being always late. He nearly missed the Florence & he
has entirely lost his chance of Dixie now So to breakfast after packing all our
traps & bidding adieu to our kind hostesses & Jimmy & Wesley we start thro
the forest with Mr Pigott & the horse in front Sterrett I & jolly little Selwin[29]
walking after. The road very wet sometimes six inches under water, not
counting the swamps wh are from 4 to 5 feet deep thro wh we had to struggle as best we could. The road lying entirely thro' forest of pine many of wh
had been tapped & skinned for Turpentine & others much burnt & charr'd.
The principal feature here was the awful cackling of the frogs wh was the
first thing roused me & it continued all thro' our Line of March [*illegible*]
after hard days walk with hot sun & very wet arrived at the Ferry & were
Hospitably entertained by Henry Ole the Black Ferry man turn in at 9.30
very tired—Sterrett & little Selwin on the floor I & our long legged N.
Carolian friend John Piggott on the only bed next the fire—They complained much of the pain of their 'poor feet' which were much swollen after
the walk. I took a jolly bath in the Wackamaw before supper to the astonish-
ment of our Friends & the nigger Ferry man—

TUESDAY, 28 FEBRUARY[30]

Started at 8 after a good breakfast of eggs & some of our own bacon friz-
zled—(We had a small barrel of provisions brought from hospitable Mrs Pigott bacon, sweet potatoes & bread wh stood us in good stead) It began
raining heavily & so continued through the day however we marched on &
came to the 1st. obstacle a river overflowing about a mile wh they call here a

[28]Signature at back of diary: "W Allen Selden Powhatan Co. Virginia." William Allen Selden,
Jr., son of Dr. William Allen Selden and Jane (Douthat) Selden, was another passenger on the
Owl (Edna Mae Selden, *Selden and Kindred of Virginia* [Richmond, 1941], p. 150).

[29]Several times Conolly misspells Selden's name.

[30]Conolly forgot to mark the date beginning this entry but noted it in the margin near the
end of this passage.

swamp This is the 7 creek swamp & there we should have been stopp'd if it had not been for a nigger whom we brought with us from the ferry who knew where the transport barge was moored & knew also as he said how to "humorate" the barge as to get thro' the trees & athwart the current so he "humorated" us across the 7 creeks & we continued our dreary march thro' the unvaried pine forest & dank sedge sometimes up to our knees & generally soppy with water after the 1st ten miles we called a halt & finding that we could not hold out for the 30 miles to the next station resolved to try & hire or buy a horse at the 1st. plantation we came to. These plantations are miserable enough & few & far between consisting of 3 or 4 fields cleared from the pine forest with the seared & charrd stumps of the pines still sticking up thro' the eye of rice field a wooden house raised on piles with 3 or 4 slave cottages barn &c. & a miserable cow & horse tethered & the well in front with its long balance pole & bucket a most cheering sight to the foot-sore traveller. We arrived at one of these habitations about 2 & went straight to the well & after a refreshing draught enquired about a horse, but theirs was so wretched he was obviously no use & the rain continued in torrents we prepared for another 20 miles of the dark wet forest—Just then arrives an old man Mr Long riding (as is the custom of the place) the horse in the shafts of his cart, who after a little parley agreed to take us 3 to Whiteville for 10 dollars. He had 6 sons in the Confed. Army who were still all alive tho' 2 had been badly wounded & had not returned to their duty He had been as he said twice married & had 14 children by his 1st wife & 5 by his second & likely says he if the war dont kill us to have 5 more In fact a fine hearty old chap with a grisly beard of a fortnights[31] growth & a Confederate great coat with a large bullet hole thro the cape & a buttoned strap at the waist so in we get & he pushes his little brown mare to a merry pace calling on friend Pigott to follow (also riding his animal), as best he can. Pigot soon cries for mercy & a more moderate pace wh old Long at length agreed to calling on him if he likes to go first. Yes my child—talking of his mare can 'lope 10 miles an hour in the saddle without the cart I often come back from Whiteville in 3 hours with her if I get any apple brandy from Jim High down there, He's my brother in law & we'll stop at His house on the way & have a drink it wont do these gentlemen any harm after the [wetting?] they have—So settle away 3 in the Long cart on straw & by Pigott after with the baggage we go to Jim Highs comfortable house with green [*illegible*] about 5 & soon found Mrs and Miss Sarah Ann a very pretty girl working at stockings & young High a friend of Selden in the same Corps who was home on furlough we soon got some apple brandy (execrable corn whiskey & tobacco & thus proceeded—to

[31]Footnote: "(Selden) (Sterrett.)."

Whiteville Railway station wh we found infested with loafers exchanging news hands in their pockets [*illegible*] we found among them Capt Byrne[32] tall military fig with one arm who at once on hearing that we were for Fayetteville volunteered to lead us on the road with his waggon we were hospitably entertained with Scoupanong wine & Tobacco by one Stanley & leaving Whiteville Ct House. at once proceeded through dark forest for [*illegible*] hours very wet & cold till the welcome sight of Mr Lemmons fire greeted us Mrs Lemmons good woman gets up & puts on her shoes & wrapper & bustles about the [*illegible*] & in about 20 mins. gets us an excellent supper, rice, bacon, eggs & syrup—whole meal bread—Old Lemmon is a regular wag in his own way. Loud complaints of the depredations of groups of deserters who steal all light articles fowls, turkeys &c—

WEDNESDAY, 1 MARCH

Next morning at 8 proceeded on our way thro' Big swamp & the interminable Forest & met only 2 invalid soldiers tired & miserable & making anxious accounts as to whether their homes had been reached by the Yanks— one poor fellow evidently dying both out of hospital & t'other an [acid?] featured fellow who grinned as he told us he had the itch a dreadful complaint wh arises from damp & [decay?] & prevails to a frightful extent in Lee's army—On for 7 hours till a comfortable Plantation offered us dinner. Mr Regan, who had 5 sons in the service one at home badly wounded on crutches The daughters buxom & engaged in making clothes the old Lady active & busy got us a Capital dinner of bacon eggs & rice in half an hour & sent us away with many kind wishes After walking 37 miles, our little horses going gaily & ineffectual [attempts?] at 2 small farmhouses, "I guess not" we were most kindly received by Mr McDonald a Presbyterian Minister—good fellow with a very nice pretty wife. We had an excellent supper of same sort & then the good Parson had prayers offers up entreaties for his countrymen in their sore distress That they might be taught Patience under their Trials & unwavering attachment to the path of duty that they might be protected from on High & have a happy issue out of all their Troubles & finally they might be taught to look beyond this life for a city wh hath foundations whose builder and maker is God After Prayers we had a good deal of pleasant talk about the incidents of the war The Lady expressing her heartfelt desire to go over to England or France any Power but the Yankee The good man expressed the same opinion with more reserve. We had excellent beds &

[32]Matthew A. Byrne (b. ca. 1839), railroad agent before the war and captain, 18th N.C. Regiment, who resigned after his left arm was amputated (*NCT*, VI, 389).

after a most comfortable sleep & excellent Bk start at 8 for Fayetteville with the kind wishes of Neill McDonald L H K McDonald[33] Rockfish Cumberland—N. Carolina—

THURSDAY, 2 MARCH[34]

We journeyed on famously with Sterrett (The experienced [*illegible*] driving & with pleasant talk about the amiable family we had left till by a deep ravine we brought up before a picket of Confederate sentries their arms bright & clean their picket hut well arranged & the remains of their watch fire They accosted us civilly enquiring news of the enemy at Wilmington as Capt Byrne wearing his grey Confed. uniform was a pass to them— shortly after we came up to an ambulance drawn by mules with 5 Confed. soldiers in it knapsacks &c & a little distance on their officer known to Selden & another curious fig in a Raccoon cap. who were in charge of these men returning to head Quarters & who had pressed the ambulance regarding the weary state of the men (in wh after our first 2 days Experience we could fully sympathize with them. Everywhere now thicken the signs of war & a little farther a half a company of joyous boys with muskets are shouting & cheering as they see the arsenal of Fayette-ville & the end of the march, & now all is bustle the wide muddy streets filled with every imaginable waggon & cart drawn generally by fair looking light horses without winkers or mules & generally the off horse carrying a nigger.[35] most of them are engaged in transporting cotton bales from the stores here to safe hiding places in the country fearing an approach Either from Sherman at Cheeraw or Wilmington. The bar-room[36] of the large Hotel is crowded with men in uniform & a fine young fellow very handsome is hobbling about on a new wooden leg with the stump still bent from the knee where the wood is attached—He was on Genl Hokes[37] staff & lost his leg at Petersburg. Mr

[33]Conolly left a space at the bottom of the page, where these signatures, not in his hand, appear.

[34]Marginal note following the signatures of W. B. Sterrett W. Allen Selden: "my fellow passengers & Friends of the march to Richmond—"

[35]Report by telegraph from Fayetteville, dated 3 March: "The Hon. Thomas Connelly, member of the British Parliament, arrived here yesterday, and took lodgings at the Fayetteville Hotel. He leaves for Richmond to-morrow. Much speculation is indulged in as to the object of his visit, but nothing reliable is known. Mr. Connelly . . . is an intelligent Irishman, well disposed towards the Confederate States" (*Richmond Whig*, 6 Mar. 1865). Similar commentary appeared in the Raleigh *Confederate* on 8 March.

[36]Signature at back of diary: "Pat Quigley Barman Fayetteville."

[37]Robert Frederick Hoke (1837–1912), major general, C.S.A. (*Gray*, pp. 140–41).

Green[38] of the Engineers made himself known to me as a nephew of the celebrated Dear [*illegible*] in Roscommon,[39] a very nice intelligent officer connected with the Arsenal here. Sterrett & I go out after dinner to see Miss Maffitt[40] & give her intelligence of her good father I make the mistake of congratulating her upon her approaching marriage, a thing never hinted at in these Latitudes but always an open question therefore a delicate one till clinched—She is very charming & retiring exceedingly pretty & amiable & very much delighted to hear of her Papa—Capital nigger Ned drove us & is highly recommended by Green for his services at the Hotel—We go over the entire arsenal a small "Enfield"[41] where they have all the most approved machinery for turning out rifles & showed us a sample with Fayetteville[42] mark a very well made handy weapon with the light Austrian ribbed Bayonet, received great attention from the officers there particularly from Sergeant Stephens[43] an Irishman from Ballinakill in Queens Co who was overjoyed to see me & came up to the Hotel & had a great talk and a glass of toddy over the old Country. Capt Green was very kind in getting our passports & every civility he could do us—Capital Tea & hot rolls & good natured buxom hostess Mrs Waddell—Add a French Maitre d'armée with his moustaches perçantes & the swagger of la Grande armée—Get a room for us 3 & to bed—

FRIDAY, 3 MARCH

Sleep well 'till 6 when Ned the darkie comes in to light the fire & tells us Bk at 1/2 past 7—Up & dress &c. After Bk get our Passports from the Prevôt Martial & go with Sterrett to see the Commander of the Arsenal Col.

[38]Footnote: "See Appendix of names." Signature at back of diary: "James Foy Greene Engr Corps C.S.A."

[39]The market town or county of that name in Ireland.

[40]Perhaps Florie Maffitt, who ran the blockade to Nassau and back on her own earlier in the war (Hamilton Cochran, *Blockade Runners of the Confederacy* [Indianapolis and New York, 1958], pp. 257–58, 274).

[41]Union and Confederate armies both used weapons modeled on the Enfield rifle musket made at the Royal Small Arms Factory, Enfield, England (*ECW*, pp. 243–44).

[42]For the Fayetteville arsenal, which used machinery the Confederates had taken from the arsenal at Harpers Ferry, Virginia, see *SHSP*, XXIV, 231–37.

[43]Footnote: "see Appendix of names." Signature at back of diary: "Thomas Stephens Sergt Fayetteville Arsenal & Armory Ballinakill, Queen's Co. Ireland" (*SHSP*, XXIV, 236).

Childe—[44] Capt Dangerfield[45] a pleasant gentleman & friend of Genl Lee took us thro' the works & then to his Qrs & introduces us to Mrs Dangerfield a quiet Ladylike person who is cheery thro' all the adverse circumstances Walk home with Dangerfield talking over the chances of the war & the possibility of licking Sherman at Cheeraw.[46] Cheeraw, Cheeraw! bet Sterrett 20 dollars that Richmond is not evacuated in 6[47] months. See the Yankee Prisoners who were recaptured last night 8 lying on the floor of a room no complaints from them They say they have been treated first rate. 3 of them were taken by a young farmer[48] near here who hearing from his little brother that there were some strange men behind the barn loaded his musket with duck Shot & call'd on them for an explanation Then told them they were his Prisoners & he would have 2 of them with his gun if necessary but if they came quietly he wl give them breakfast & take them to the Prevôt Martial here wh he did riding his horse & halting them all when one stopped for a minute— Brought them safe in While questioning these Prisoners as to where they had escaped from &c I asked whether any was Irish, to wh a fine fellow replied waal my mother was Rhode Island and my father New hampshire so I am a downright Yankee there's no doubt I found one fellow in the Arsenal who had come from the Yankees & bore an excellent character as a workman who turned out to be Wm Allen of Kinockbrick near Raphoe[49] nephew of Robt Allen. I gave him a gold peice of 2 1/2 dollars. We then visited the Hospital under the care of Dr Fessenden[50] who showed us some extraordinary cases of wounds one under the arm coming thro' the chest & out under the left breast, another thro' the neck where he said the most experienced surgeon could hardly pass a Knife without touching some vital point & yet both these with many others we saw were doing well with every prospect of recovery but there was one case so extraordinary[51] that I asked Dr Fes-

[44]Frederick Lynn Childs (1831–1894), West Point graduate and Confederate commander of the Fayetteville arsenal (Samuel A. Ashe and Stephen B. Weeks, eds., *Biographical History of North Carolina...*, VII [Greensboro, N.C., 1908], pp. 60–66).

[45]Captain J. E. P. Dangerfield, military storekeeper and paymaster of the Fayetteville arsenal (*SHSP*, XXIV, 237).

[46]As Conolly wrote this, Federal troops were entering Cheraw, South Carolina, near the North Carolina border and on 5 March prepared to move toward Fayetteville (*Almanac*, pp. 646–48).

[47]Footnote: "Bet with Sterrett."

[48]Footnote: "Carry a young lad of 16 near Fayetteville 8 miles."

[49]A market town in Co. Donegal, Conolly's parliamentary constituency.

[50]Surgeon B. F. Fessenden, chief medical officer at general hospital number 6 in Fayetteville (*Confederate States Medical & Surgical Journal*, I, no. 9 [1864], 152).

[51]Footnote: "See full report in Appx."

senden for a full report of it to send to "the Lancet"[52] on my return to England, there were in almost every ward Ladies attending on the sick with their little baskets of comforts according to the diet prescribed on the board at the head of each bed—The town was full of men bearing honorable marks of the war in maimed limbs & young lads bearing arms these are called the details & are regularly drilled till capable of taking the field with the regulars receiving no pay or clothing 'till then.

SATURDAY, 4 MARCH

We hear confused accts from the front at Cheeraw on which no reliance can be placed some stating that there has been an engagement & Sherman whipped, others that Hardee[53] has been outflanked by him & that he is in possession of Cheeraw, but the official orders to remove all cotton & valuables & the constant throng of mule & horse teams with loaded wagons taking the effects of the citizens to a place of greater security & the fact that the most valuable machinery has already been transported inland from the Arsenal, all look very like the Yankee advance we stir ourselves to procure means of transport to Raleigh but find all the horses pressed for these more urgent duties & on trying whether we could make our way by Egypt by rail & thence on we find that all the horses there also have been taken up by the Govt & several passengers have returned from there having been unable to proceed.

So we make the best of it & order a banjo band & some whiskey to our room & ask all the wounded officers about & have a capital evenings amusement up to 1 o'clock dancing & singing & negro music being kept up with occasional refreshing draughts of the [*illegible*].

Mem: a very handsome & gentlemanlike fellow Capt. Justice[54] who had lost a leg he belongs to Genl Hoke's staff & was at Wilmington attack—

We left Fayetteville at 2.30 having got one horse lent us by Col. Pemberton[55] & bought another for 3,000 dollars Confederate money equal to about £10 so hiring a nigger to bring back Pemberton's horse & carriage we start along a very bad road sometimes up to the axels in mud for the House of a Col macneil to whom we bear Introduction from Pemberton who is a trump & after regaling us sends us on our way with the assurance that his friend will forward us to Raleigh next day—we arrive at Col. McNeils hospi-

---

[52]A leading British medical periodical.

[53]William Joseph Hardee (1815–1873), lieutenant general, C.S.A. (*Gray*, pp. 124–25).

[54]Lt. J. G. Justice, A.D.C. on the staff of Maj. Gen. Robert F. Hoke (*CSO*, p. 88).

[55]John Clifford Pemberton (1814–1881), lieutenant general when he surrendered at Vicksburg, at the end of the war served as artillery lieutenant colonel (*Gray*, pp. 232–33).

table home at 10 p.m & get an excellent supper & beautiful white beds Luxury! There are 2 soldiers also taken in by this most excellent gentleman for the night being on their way home having been Prisoners since the battle of Gettysburg[56] & now discharged on parole. Coil ourselves up & thanking the good Col. wish him goodnight

SUNDAY, 5 MARCH

   Meet all the good Col's family at Bk at 7.30 Eldest Edward a fine boy just going to join his regt at Petersburg 5 smaller 3 girls, I never saw so good a breakfast of farm produce the Hominy, the buns the crumpets, the sausages, the fried bacon & eggs the delicious milk the sweet potatoes & the old Lady was very proud of the neatness of the service & had her black girls in great order with their quaint white caps & large rolling eyes—Capital glass of brandy with the gay old Col. who is a great farmer & after a promise of some turnip seed from England we get into his carriage drawn by a nice pair of greys & start for Raleigh on the way & while our carriage is ploughing thro some of the worst ground we meet Genl Joe Johnston[57] riding with his Staff & had a short talk with him He is a [light?] shaped [little?] man, with good address & very quiet manner asked 2 or 3 questions about the road we recommend him to Col. McNeils & tell him how well we were treated He was followed by an ambulance drawn by 4 mules containing his camp equipage & his own camp wagon with a splendid pair of bays & 2 led horses He bade us a courteous adieu & bon voyage!—Arrive at Raleigh very hungry at 9. p.m & can get nothing to eat every place being shut because of Sunday & the fires being all out & the Cooks gone away! Poor little Selden who has been up to this as merry as a cricket meets his cousin here who tells him for the 1st time of his father's death which occurred nearly 2 months back but wh he had not heard at Nassau He is very much shocked by it, & I fear poor little fellow is left almost penniless the Yankees having destroyed all his father's fine property & a large family younger than him he only 19 Poor little fellow! I pity him from my soul & so does good Sterrett who is a regular Trump!!!. Trumps are scarce these times—

[56]Footnote: "Gettysburg was fought 1st July 1863."
[57]Joseph Eggleston Johnston (1807–1891), general, C.S.A., was assigned in February 1865 to oppose Sherman's march north (*Gray*, pp. 161–62).

MONDAY, 6 MARCH

Up at 7 and hearty breakfast to make up for the want of a supper. Go out to see the place Coln McCrea[58] Editor of "the Confederate" son of old Major McCrea of Fayetteville a very fine erect old man with a clear eye who remembered Lafayette's entrance into Fayetteville. Col. McCrea is a zealous Patriot and his Paper is True to the Cause tho' there is a disaffected party here He is also a very pleasant man & has the character of a good Public speaker. Great exertions are being make here by the Govr Vance[59] & his staff to raise contributions of provisions from every person in the county all of which are brought with the [*illegible*] stores here & all the horses & mules, large houses are being impressed for hospitals & all preparations made for a Campaign in the neighborhood hear of Mr. Vitzetelly[60] the celebrated draughtsman Correspondent of the Illt London News & find him in the apartment of Messr Colley's agent Mr Stringer[61] a very clever business young man, one of the smartest I have seen. Vizetelly is charming, of great experience capital narrator & as for Pencil "of world-wide fame." We became great friends & he put me up to Lawley,[62] Portman[63] &c as Litterary attaché to the army of Virginia besides telling us numerous stirring tales of Camp & Field from the Battle of Chickamauga & the huge dinner with old Preston & Genl

[58]Duncan Kirkland McRae (1820–1888), lawyer, politician, C.S.A. colonel, North Carolina trade envoy to Europe, and editor of the Raleigh *Confederate*. His father, John McRae, had been a Fayetteville postmaster and editor (*DAB*, XII, 164–65).

[59]Zebulon Baird Vance (1830–1894), North Carolina congressman before the war and, as governor (1862–65), one of the most effective southern state leaders (*DAB*, XIX, 158–61).

[60]Fellow student in France with Gustave Doré, draughtsman and war correspondent for the *Illustrated London News*, Frank Vizetelly (1830–1883?) was with Hicks Pasha's Egyptian army when the Mahdi annihilated it in the Sudan (*DNB*, XX, 386; W. Stanley Hoole, *Vizetelly Covers the Confederacy*, Confederate Centennial Studies, no. 4 [Tuscaloosa, Ala., 1957]).

[61]Signature at back of diary: "Henry E. Stringer," an agent in the blockade-running business employed by various London firms, including Messrs. Collie & Co. See *ORN*, ser. ii, II, 483–85; *OR*, ser. iv, II, 525–26.

[62]Former M.P. and private secretary to William E. Gladstone, Francis Charles Lawley (1825–1901) was the London *Times* correspondent covering the Civil War (William Stanley Hoole, *Lawley Covers the Confederacy*, Confederate Centennial Studies, no. 26 [Tuscaloosa, 1964], pp. 9–25). Conolly expected to meet Lawley in America. Although on opposite benches, the two may have known one another from the Commons. Appendix: "Lawleys introductory Letter Richmond."

[63]Maurice Berkeley Portman (1833–1888), third son of viscount Portman and aide to Wade Hampton (1818–1902), lieutenant general, C.S.A. (*Gray*, pp. 122–23; *Burke's Peerage* [1938], p. 2001; C. Vann Woodward, ed., *Mary Chesnut's Civil War* [New Haven and London, 1981], p. 771. Woodward's footnote on p. 771 erroneously called him A. P. Portman).

Cheatham[64] after it, to the feu d'enfer of sixty vessels poured with fatal accuracy on the [devoted?] Fort Fisher the other day both of which with all the intervening fights he witnessed. Not a sparrow could have existed on the parapet of Fort Fisher & not a gun remained that was not dismounted by the terrible storm of heavy artillery The fall of Fisher reflects no discredit on the garrison, who after all the firing defended it with desperate gallantry [*illegible*] & repulsed 1st Assault.[65] He thinks the Yankee gunnery very formidable!—Pay a visit to Govr Vance[66] in his office in the Capitol & find him going thro' the duties of his State hunting up deserters, arranging transport, impressing houses, waggons horses, & niggers, raising provisions, organizing committees & superintending his Home Guard add to all this he has to attend a mass meeting at Hillsborough[67] 90 miles away tomorrow & tho ably seconded by Col. McCrea who goes with him has even in this Eleventh hour of the war & with the enemy at the gate to listen in public meeting to men who [still?] entertain Yankee predelictions & advocate return to the hated Union. He is a fine specimen of a true son of the soil—Walk all over the town wh is well built in rectangular streets & pleasantly situated on the side of a hill topped by the Capitol, a handsome building of Doric architectr in white sandstone. Good dinner at the Yerborough House[68] & cigar with Stringer & Vizetelly & then go to pay our respects to Govr Vance &c & invited by him to go in his carriage with Col McCrea on our way 'on to Richmond— Vizetelly goes with us to Mr & Mrs Barringer[69] old friends of Sir R. Pakenham[70] & she of the Empress Eugenie[71] long time ago in Spain—I promise to send her a print of the Empss when I get home—He is a quaint old man & both are quite gentle-folk—as Stringer says a reel Lady!—Embark on board

[64]The battle of Chickamauga took place 19–20 September 1863. Conolly met Brig. Gen. William Preston (1816–1887) at Nassau. Cheatham was probably Benjamin Franklin Cheatham (1820–1886), major general, C.S.A. (*Gray*, pp. 246, 47–48).

[65]The Confederates drove off the first Federal attack on Fort Fisher at Christmas 1864.

[66]Appendix: "Governor Vances Address to N. Carolina—slaves admitted to ranks of Army Bill passed."

[67]About half the distance from Raleigh to Greensboro.

[68]The Yarborough House, a leading Raleigh hotel.

[69]Signature at back of diary: "D. M. Barringer Raleigh N.C." Daniel Moreau Barringer (1806–1873), diplomat, congressman, and adviser to North Carolina Confederate officials. His wife was Elizabeth (Wethered) Barringer, of Baltimore (*DAB*, I, 648–49).

[70]Conolly's uncle, Sir Richard Pakenham (1797–1868), former minister to the United States and Portugal (*DNB*, XV, 85).

[71]When Barringer was minister to Spain (1849–53), he and his wife apparently met Eugénie Marie de Montijo de Guzmán, Comtesse de Teba and later wife of Napoleon III. The empress' Irish grandmother was a neighbor of the Conollys. A frequent visitor to Paris, Conolly became friends with Napoleon III.

the "Cars" at 12.30 and after a rough journey in filthy carriages alleviated by the jokes & broad humor of Governor Vance arrive at Greensboro'[72] at 8.30 am

TUESDAY, 7 MARCH

Get a most wretched breakfast close to Railway & when I told the Lady presiding my opinion of it she flouted out in high dudgeon & the Master rushed for his Pistol & would have cut up ferocious had not Sterrett interfered & calmed the fury of the dame & the impetuosity of the Lord who without speaking contented himself with glaring at me as tho' anxious to devour me without salt We started out for a walk thro' Greensboro' wh is a rising little Place where 4 lines of Railway meet & where even now they are building largely.—Whole place full of soldiers in all manner of garb, Prisoners returning on parole & all the strays & waifs of war. Waggons with mule teams & black drivers & soldiers on duty keeping order & [regularity?] & the big blunderbuss funnelled Engines booming & ringing their alarm bells at all hours—Cars full inside with motley troops armed & covered with picturesque crowds camping on the top & rolling themselves in their large blankets with nothing but beards & sloughhat & rifle protruding &—&c—&— Such all covered & spattered with red mud wh marks everything & every body here was the scene we left at Greensboro when by arrangement of Genl Wilcox[73] we left in baggage train wh gets in time for the passenger train at Danville 70 miles done in 6 hours such a [crush?] in a dark waggon! women & children crying and doing other things, Soldiers smoking all pell mell sitting as best we could on the baggage & passing round an occasional bottle of vile Spirits by the dim light of a [*illegible*] light fixed to the centre post where stood also a bucket of water & some hollow gourds to drink out of, We arrived at Danville—& then with much bustle for the baggage got into the Guards Van of the Passenger train the cars being already full when we got there & a whole crowd left in the moonlight to wait till the morning baggage train—Very glad to get a quiet nook in the Luggage room of Guards van to make myself quite comfortable on a large box abounding in big-headed nails & slept so delightfully that no feather bed could have induced better slumber

[72]About 65 miles west of Raleigh.

[73]Maj. Gen. Cadmus Marcellus Wilcox (1824–1890) (*Gray*, pp. 337–38). Vance introduced Wilcox to Conolly and asked him to see the M.P. safely to Richmond. Wilcox described Conolly as "this genial and warm-hearted stranger" who "was eccentric in the dress he wore on the streets and about camp. He had all the vivacity, and much of the wit and humor peculiar to his race" (*SHSP*, IV, 21n–22n).

CHAPTER TWO

"OH BUT YOU SHOULD SEE IT IN THE SUMMER!"

WEDNESDAY, 8 MARCH[1]

Arrived at Richmond at 2 p.m & set down in my red breeches, sea boots & flannel shirt to the first real dinner in Dixie, Sterrett finds friends & acquaintances everywhere & Wilcox knows all the General officers—Dress clean & go up to pay my respects to dear Old Mrs Mason[2]—& her daughters & neices Dear old Lady! Plucky dear old Lady She had just received her Son who had been on Genl Early's staff in the engagement of last week when the whole of his force of 1100 men & all his artillery were surprized & Captured by Sheridan on the Lynchburg road[3] Young Mason barely escaping with his life across the river thro' the Yankee fire She does not dispair The aspect of Richmond at this time is wretched Shops with nothing in them except enough to show how miserably they are run out Stores with open doors & empty bales & broken up packing cases & dirty straw "A beggarly account of Empty boxes"[4] The streets full of all manner description character & phases of the

---

[1]On 7 March the *Richmond Whig*, which a day earlier had noted a telegraphed report on Conolly's arrival in Fayetteville, stated that "the Hon. Thomas Conolly, of Donegal . . . is daily expected."

[2]On 25 March Conolly received a dinner invitation from "Mr. Ambler Mrs. Masons son in law." Thus it is likely that Mrs. Mason was Elizabeth (Chew) Mason, whose daughter had married John Ambler and whose husband was James Murray Mason, senator from Virginia before the war and Confederate emissary to Great Britain. Conolly might have met Mason because of the latter's lobbying efforts (*DAB*, XII, 364–65).

[3]At Waynesboro, Virginia, on 2 March troops of Brig. Gen. George A. Custer, part of the army of Maj. Gen. Philip Henry Sheridan, defeated those of Lt. Gen. Jubal Anderson Early (*Almanac*, p. 645).

[4]A comparison of Richmond's stores with the apothecary shop from which Romeo bought poison: "and about his shelves/ A beggarly account of empty boxes,/ Green earthen pots, blad-

human species knots of rowdies,[5] rustic & urbane in all habiliments inter-
spersed with in every image of [*illegible*]—dubious—dull—sparkling—
moody furious—[wild?] mad, raving or stupid intoxication—pickets of mud-
stained-slough-hatted rawboned cavalry—Every species of grey, brown,
fresh, threadbare, jaunty & ragged uniform, or rather multiform here & there
with smart officers & grisly hard lined determined veterans always neat
among their rough & uncouth Comrades (as yet untutored in the ways of
war), mud, mud, mud everywhere even thro' the halls and corridors of the
hotel[6] which are a babel of chatter & oaths the word Yankee, & Yanks issuing
from every group [few?] women in streets & those of the better class generally in mourning but a total absence of those wretched miserables who generally follow our European camps.[7] The situation of the city is magnificent, it
occupies a hill on a bend of the James River which runs in wild torrents
round it divided into several rapid streams by islands or sand mounds covered with [*illegible*] & sedge—the opposite side being rocky & handsomely
wooded[8] with oak & Pine The Capitol[9] stands on the crown of the principal
hill & the two principal streets Main St & broad Street are parallel up two
sloping valleys at either side of the principal hills there is a farther hill of less
size Church Hill & the Streets running at right angles to the 2 leading
thorofares [have?] a fine effect in descending the great hill & passing the valley in straight lines & up the other hill to the horizon

THURSDAY, 9 MARCH

The hotel is of vast size now miserably furnished scarcely anything in the
bedrooms except the beds & a few broken chairs, all the carpets having been
sent (& this is also the case of private houses) to the military stores to be cut
up for army blankets, there are even coats made out of odds & ends of these
same carpets [*illegible*] wh have saved many a poor fellows life on Picket &

---

ders and musty seeds,/ Remnants of packthread and old cakes of roses,/ Were thinly scatter'd, to
make up a show./ Noting this penury, to myself I said/ 'An if a man did need a poison now,/
Whose sale is present death in Mantua,/ Here lives a caitiff wretch would sell it him' " (*Romeo
and Juliet* Act V, Sc. 1, Lines 44–52).

[5]Footnotes: "Shallotte to Wackamaw Ferry 25 to Whiteville 28 to Big Swamp 19 to Rockfish
28 to Fayetteville 10 [total] 110" and "to Fayetteville 110 to Raleigh 63 to Greensboro' 100
Danville 60 Richmond 140 Total miles 473."

[6]A marginal note identifies the hotel as the Spotswood, Main and Eighth Sts.

[7]This observation, admittedly made on Conolly's first day in the city, is not borne out by
most studies of wartime Richmond, the best of which is Emory M. Thomas, *The Confederate
State of Richmond: A Biography of the Capital* (Austin and London, 1971).

[8]Marginal note: "voir the map of Richmond."

[9]Thomas Jefferson's Virginia state capitol, completed in 1792, dominated the city skyline.

outpost duty (for these pickets and outposts have been now kept up around this hero city with [unrelenting?] vigilance for the last 3 years. Almost all the crockery in the Hotel is cracked & broken & we had to buy 3 tumblers for our room at 25 dollars each—60 dollars for a bottle of brandy & so on—

Nevertheless we eat good strong fare in abundance & have plenty of water as long as the James River is not dried up by the Yankees, like the hosts of Alexander & we have very pleasant companions in the heroine Southern Ladies[10] who have taken refuge here from Savanah Wilmington, Charleston, & the lately burned Columbia Damn Sherman![11]—The streets are lined with trees like the Boulevards & the Virginians still in its forlorn condition exult in the beauty of their unconquered city & say Oh but you should see it in the summer! God knows if it will ever see another summer—! Sherman near Fayetteville, Terry & Scholefield marching for Goldsboro from Wilmington to join him Sheridan threatening on the N. in the Valley Fredericksburg Thomas coming from Tenessee & threatening Bristol & Grant with 150,000 men investing the city on the S[12] yet these earnest people talk of seeing their favorite city when the leaves are out!

FRIDAY, 10 MARCH[13]

A light thro' the darkness! A telegram announces[14] the first Victory for the Confederates! Bragg[15] has checked the Wilmington corps marching on

[10]A resident of the Ballard House Hotel wrote that "The drawing room was again crowded last night [9 Mar.], and we got up an important dance on the spur of the moment. General Kershaw, General Gary, and General Ruggles were present; also our friends, the congressman, the captain, the major, and the M. P. Oh! yes. We know Mr. Connelly, an Irish M.P. and Southern sympathizer. He seems to have plenty of money, and lives here in great style for war times" (diary of Malvina Black Gist, in Katharine M. Jones, ed., *Heroines of Dixie: Confederate Women Tell Their Story of the War* [Indianapolis and New York, 1955], p. 380).

[11]The burning of Columbia, South Carolina, was an issue of dispute between Maj. Gen. William Tecumseh Sherman, U.S.A., and Lt. Gen. Wade Hampton, C.S.A. Appendix: "Genl Wade Hampton's reply to Sherman."

[12]Union generals Alfred Howe Terry (1827–1890), John McAllister Schofield (1831–1906), George Henry Thomas (1816–1870), and Ulysses Simpson Grant (1822–1885) (*Blue*, pp. 497–98, 425–26, 500–502, 183–86).

[13]Beside the date Conolly wrote "Day of Fasting & Humiliation." The government had declared 10 March a "day of public humiliation, fasting and prayer" (*Richmond Whig*, 12 Mar. 1865). Appendix: "Papers of Confederacy Davis Proclamation of Fast day Lee's Genl order [*illegible*]."

[14]Apppendixes: "Telegram recd at Richmond Mar. 8 1865" and "Official announcement of Action ditto—"

[15]Braxton Bragg (1817–1876), general, C.S.A. (*Gray*, pp. 30–31). The *Richmond Dispatch* of 10 March announced this minor Confederate success.

Cadmus Marcellus Wilcox (1824–1890), the Confederate general who met Conolly in Raleigh and accompanied him to Richmond. *Virginia Historical Society*

In his first visit to a service at St. Paul's Church in Richmond, Conolly described "the marked head & clearly chisled features" of Confederate President Jefferson Davis (1808–1889), who appears here in this rarely seen postwar photograph taken by Michael Miley. *Miley Collection, Virginia Historical Society*

Goldsboro' at Kingston N.C & taken artillery & 1500 prisoners—This is invaluable as giving Joe Johnston breathing time to concentrate on Sherman before the latter is reinforced he is still reported 70,000 strong. R.E. Lee—

Breakfast by invitation with Mr & Mrs Pratt, Mrs Helme[16] sis to Mrs Abe Lincoln & Mrs Brown[17] pretty Mrs Brown (Jimmy's[18] cousin) self Genl Wilcox & the invaluable Sterrett.

Go to St Pauls Ch[19] with Mrs Brown & another pretty woman Mrs Clay[20] & hear the finest war Sermon I ever heard—The entire congregation fall on their knees to join in Prayer with the Eloquent Preacher[21] at the [Peroration?] of his discourse—I give 40 dollars in gold & dear old Sterrett a like sum for the Collection, the bags are filled with the contributions which are to go to the wounded & sick!

Prominent among the crowd in the centre of the Church was the marked head & clearly chisled features of Jeff. Davis[22] his hair quite grey & his lantern jaws more thin & sallow than of old but his grey eyes bright & clear showing that altho toil & watchfulness had told upon his physical strength the lustre of his Spirit is undimmed—!

We took a walk in the Evening in Franklin St The fashionable promenade but with the exception of our party Mrs Brown & self Genl Wilcox & the widow the street was deserted no one feeling inclined on *this* day to appear in Public—

[16]Emily (Todd) Helm, widow of Brig. Gen. Benjamin Hardin Helm, C.S.A., and half-sister of Mary (Todd) Lincoln (*Gray*, pp. 132–33; *ECW*, pp. 356–57).

[17]Josephine (Lovett) Brown (1835–1915), a friend of Confederate Senator Clement C. Clay, Jr., and his wife, Virginia Caroline (Tunstall) Clay. As a courier associated with Clay's clandestine intelligence operations, Brown had arrived in Richmond on her latest trip from the North one day before Conolly. See entry for 22 March (H. L. Clay to C. C. Clay, 8 Mar. 1865 and Josephine Brown to C. C. Clay, 18 Mar. 1865, Clay Papers, NA).

[18]Appendix: "Poplin dress for _____."

[19]St. Paul's Episcopal Church, corner of Grace and Ninth Sts., west side of Capitol Square, built 1845.

[20]Harriet Celestia (Comer) Clay, sister-in-law of Confederate senator Clement C. Clay, Jr. When Conolly met her, he was in the company of Josephine Brown, a courier in the secret network run by Senator Clay.

[21]Footnote: "Revd. Mr. Sprague of the 'Southern Churchman.' " Dr. Daniel Francis Sprigg (1824–1908) was rector of Holy Trinity Church and editor of the *Southern Churchman.*

[22]Jefferson Davis (1808–1889), Mississippi planter, U.S. secretary of war and senator, and only president of the Confederacy.

Go to tea with W. P. Burwell[23] whom we find in bed whence without drawers he begins a lengthened argument on the Slave question wh is only slightly interrupted by his drawers, his stockings, pants, boots, false collar, & shakes his fingers thro' his hair & shrug into his coat & we proceed to the Parlour where Mrs. Brander a hard featured old [owl?] presides at excellent oyster collation tea & muffins—More Eloquence incoherent, inconclusive but rapid & vehement & much relief when relief arrives in the shape of 5 young ladies Miss Brander being the only very pretty one who sing to a discordant harpsicord We thank them gallantly for their Music & beat a retreat to bed. Cocktails

SATURDAY, 11 MARCH

Breakfast party as usual Mr & Mrs Pratt Mrs B. Sterrett widow Helme Genl Wilcox & self—Up to Myers[24] & then wait all day on Jeff. Davis who is engaged with his Cabinet discussing Genl Hoods[25] report—Introduced to his staff Col Johnston s. of Genl Sidney Johnston killed at Shiloh.[26] Col Wood.[27] Col: Lubbock[28] formerly Governor of Texas & Capt Goree[29] of Longstreets[30] staff Col Johnston a fine fellow offers me his horse to ride whenever I like[31]—Then up to Senate to see Judge Oldham[32] & other Patres

[23]William P. Burwell (b.1828), lawyer, colonel, C.S.A. (Joseph Van Holt Nash, *Students of the University of Virginia* . . . [Baltimore, 1878]). The Richmond city directory for 1860 lists a J. S. R. Burwell boarding with a Mrs. Louisiana Brander on Franklin St.

[24]Probably attorney and publisher Gustavus Adolphus Myers (1801–1869). See footnote for 28 March entry.

[25]John Bell Hood (1831–1879), general, C.S.A. (*Gray*, pp. 142–43).

[26]William Preston Johnston (1831–1899), an aide to Davis. See Arthur Marvin Shaw, *William Preston Johnston: A Transitional Figure of the Confederacy* (Baton Rouge, 1943).

[27]John Taylor Wood (1830–1904), a grandson of Zachary Taylor, nephew of Jefferson Davis's first wife, an aide to Davis, and commander of the commerce raider CSS *Tallahassee*. See Royce Gordon Shingleton, *John Taylor Wood: Sea Ghost of the Confederacy* (Athens, Ga., 1979).

[28]Francis Richard Lubbock (1815–1905) Confederate governor of Texas and later an aide to Davis (Ralph A. Wooster, "Texas," in W. Buck Yearns, ed., *The Confederate Governors* [Athens, Ga., 1985], pp. 199–208).

[29]Thomas Jewett Goree (1835–1905), an aide to Longstreet throughout the war (Langston James Goree V, ed., *The Thomas Jewett Goree Letters*, Vol. I, *The Civil War Correspondence* . . . [Bryan, Tex., 1981], pp. i–iv).

[30]James Longstreet (1821–1904), lieutenant general, C.S.A. (*Gray*, pp. 192–93).

[31]Appendix: "Col. Johnstons A.D.C. letter offering horse."

[32]Williamson Simpson Oldham (1813–1868), of Arkansas and later Texas, was one of the most diligent Confederate legislators in Richmond (*BDC*, pp. 333–34).

conscripti.[33] Henry of Va[34] Hunter The Peacemaker[35] & others. These men strike an Englishman much from their uncouth exterior, untrimmed beards, shaggy hair &c. but when once in conversation are able, pleasant, even brilliant & universally civil & polite—Congress a tax Bill on transfers of Property of all Kinds (regular Gladstone)[36] approved because of the necessity of the state but otherwise much objected to—Dinner as usual—Walk with Mrs B. & Sterrett—Tea party[37] at Genl Andersons[38] very pleasant folk & charming daughter of Mason formerly at Paris[39] young Mrs Anderson family & young widow in deep mourning—Alarm bell ringing all night & City Guards all turn out! Oh nothing new! only the Yanks appearing within a short distance of the town[40]—Oh Thats all—go to bed immediately—

SUNDAY, 12 MARCH

To Church at St Pauls with Mrs Brown & Sterrett & then to pay some visits with Mr Burwell. Mrs Lee[41] Miss Agnes Lee[42] & . . . &c. Dinner with same party & then receive visitors in our Room Mr Portman who has had varied fortunes in this Country & has lately been with Genl Wade Hampton & Mr T.

[33]Patres conscripti were the senators of ancient Rome.

[34]The Second Confederate Congress did not include a Virginia member named Henry, nor did the 1865 Virginia General Assembly. Perhaps Conolly meant Gustavus Adolphus Henry (1804–1880), Confederate senator from Tennessee (*BRCC*, pp. 116–17).

[35]Former senator from Virginia Robert Mercer Taliaferro Hunter (1809–1887) represented his state in the Confederate Senate and was a member of the abortive peace commission of February 1865 (*DAB*, IX, 403–5).

[36]See Frank E. Vandiver, ed., "Proceedings of the Second Confederate Congress . . . ," *SHSP*, LII. Conolly naturally made a comparison with British politics, where Chancellor of the Exchequer William E. Gladstone had established a reputation for financial virtuosity. Conolly's comment suggests that, as a good Tory, he took a jaundiced view of such agility.

[37]Footnote: "Tea party Col. Fitzhugh Judge Oldham 5 Andersons & Genl self Sterrett Wilcox Cap. B——."

[38]Brig. Gen. Joseph Reid Anderson (1813–1892) had made the Tredegar Iron Works the centerpiece of Confederate war production. See Charles B. Dew, *Ironmaker to the Confederacy . . .* (New Haven and London, 1966).

[39]In 1859 Mary Ann Mason, daughter of the U.S. minister to France, John Young Mason, had married Archer Anderson, son of Joseph Reid Anderson (*OB*, No. 31 [Oct. 1975], 3).

[40]Perhaps a reference to the appearance of Federal cavalry at Goochland Court House, on their way from the Shenandoah Valley to join the army besieging Petersburg (*Almanac*, p. 651).

[41]Mary Anna Randolph (Custis) Lee (1808–1873), daughter of George Washington Parke Custis and great-granddaughter of Martha Washington, had married Robert E. Lee in 1831.

[42]Eleanor Agnes Lee (1841–1873), fifth of the Lees' seven children.

Sneed[43] a friend of his & a good sort together with Mr Burwell & Genl Harris[44] make a round of cocktails Then out with Burwell to see the Parade of charming Ladies in Franklin St The chosen walk of Richmond Belles see them all Mrs Pres. Davis[45] & her sister[46] heading the van—Home to tea & pleasant visit from old FitzHugh[47] a real thoroug-going Tory for Established Church & ranks & orders "on principle" This dreadful crisis has opened many mens eyes to the value of stable governments & strong checks upon the wicked nature of man—His discourse on the sound Public opinion & moral character of the South. promises me a Copy of his Book—Fine old man! argument with the Ladies in the Parlour in which I am beaten & they will not have the idea of ranks & classes tho' they have their darkies as a lower & the whites as completely an aristocratic class as ever the Helots & Athenians of old represented—Genl Willcox makes his adieux, to his post tomorrow! & Portman is to occupy his place & bed in our Room No. 60 The Mars Hill of Richmond in wh the wise men of the East receive & teach!!![48]

MONDAY, 13 MARCH

Up 7. Breakfast with Ladies as usual. Then to get passports from the Prevôt Marshall & Major Norris[49] [*illegible*] head of the Secret Police & Signal corps a real crafty fellow with a horrid squint. Then to leave my name at the Presidents office with Col. Lubbock & to call at his private house at 9 tonight.—

[43]As his signature at the back of the diary indicates, "T. Sneed" was Thomas Lowndes Snead (1828–1890), a Virginian who had moved to Missouri and was elected to the Second Confederate Congress (*BDC*, p. 395).

[44]Signature at back of diary: "Genl. Thos. A. Harris Hannibal Missouri." "A celebrated *bon vivant*," and thus an ideal companion for Conolly, former Confederate legislator Thomas Alexander Harris (1826–1895) was still using his military rank in the Missouri State Guard (*BDC*, pp. 218–19; *BRCC*, pp. 109–10).

[45]Varina (Howell) Davis (1826–1906), second wife of Jefferson Davis.

[46]Margaret Graham (Howell) de Stoess (b.1842), Mrs. Davis's younger sister.

[47]George Fitzhugh (1806–1881). The book he promised was *Sociology for the South, or The Failure of Free Society* (Richmond, 1854) or *Cannibals All! or, Slaves Without Masters* (Richmond, 1857). See *DAB*, VI, 437–38 and Drew Gilpin Faust, *A Sacred Circle: The Dilemma of the Intellectual in the Old South, 1840–1860* (Baltimore and London, 1977).

[48]Footnote: "Clean up my ancient Pistolet & oil her locks write up my books & make arrangements for the camp!!!—on Tuesday—!! T.C."

[49]William Norris (1820–1896), head of the covert Secret Service Bureau, part of the Confederate Signal Corps (David Winfred Gaddy, "William Norris and the Confederate Signal and Secret Service," *MHM*, LXX [1975], 167–88).

Conolly called Major William Norris (1820–
1896), head of the Confederate intelligence service, "a real crafty fellow with a horrid squint."
Valentine Museum, Richmond, Virginia

On Col. Johnstons mare vixen to see Longstreets Corps close to the town
his faithful Irish servant, Maurice Kavanagh.[50] "For all the world like the old
counthry *'some o thems bad & more of thems worse'*—The great extent of
His Lines seem to be carefully laid out & backed by a second & third line of
defences & forts He has 40,000 men & telegraph wires communicating with
Lee & Secty at war[51] little Goree showed me all over with great civility. Dinner at Mr Pizzini's[52] Mrs Brown Mr & Mrs Pratt, T. Sneed—Portman Mrs

[50]A note at the back of the diary identified him as Longstreet's stud groom from Wexford,
Ireland.
[51]Secretary of war Maj. Gen. John C. Breckinridge. See entry for 21 March.
[52]To Mary Chesnut, Pizzini's was "that very best of Italian confectioners" (Woodward, ed.,
Mary Chesnut's Civil War, p. 164). The Pizzinis seemed to have had a monopoly on the business
according to the 1860 city directory, with three members of the family running confectionary
shops at three Richmond locations.

On several occasions Connolly visited the Davises at home in the Richmond house that became known as the White House of the Confederacy, seen here in a photograph taken at the turn of the century. *Virginia Historical Society*

Helme Sterrett & I—Oysters fried—Champagne &c 15,00 dollars about £4.16. for 8 persons 12/each. Up to Pres. Davis in the Evg and spend 2 hours with his family evg very pleasant.

President Davis is a very remarkable man! His quiet manner & ready easy conversation with his clearly chisled shave face & grey eye & thin lips aquiline nose mask a man of extraordinary determination The quiet of his adress amounts to mildness & he never by accident lets fall an uncharitable expression of anybody—His presense is very dignified & reminds one by its quick active movement of some French General in presence of Napoleon[53]—He makes a series of slight bows with his head when stating any proposition & is in all respects a graceful, spirited gentleman—His conversation is easy, copious in illustration from foreign countries & rich & animated.! In the course

[53]In August 1863 Conolly had been a guest of Napoleon III at the military camp at Chalons-sur-Marne.

of conversation I alluded to the fearful malignity & magnitude of the war For the first I was entirely prepared I knew if it was to be a war it would be one of bitterest animosity but I never calculated upon its reaching such gigantic proportions I never saw quiet determination more strikingly manifest in any person than in Jeff. Davis—Mrs. Davis is a very different character a great talker & very bitter she is calculated to damage any cause however good Her coarse features & masculine figure are destructive of all the prestige belonging to Ladies & when she opens fire wh she is sure to do on the earliest opportunity & indulges in a succession of clever (for she is very quick) smart sneers against some nice Lady like Mrs Clay then indeed she is intolerable—Miss Maggie Howell her sister is a nice girl tant soit peu affected but a good talker & gentle withal unexceptionable waist—pretty foot very! I went several evenings to pay my respects to Jeff. who commanded my respect but always avoided the tigress & generally found the Evg End with a pleasant laugh with Miss Maggie Howell—Jeff. seems to be entirely impressed with the awful destinies wh he is wielding & yet never desponds, never says a word against the scoundrels who are continually carping at him & opposing him or against the lukewarm except to allude to them as rather weak-kneed—

TUESDAY, 14 MARCH

Up rather later & it was 1/2 past 8 before I got my breakfast & owing perhaps to the copious entertainments of strangers in our Room last night. Portman being now duly installed in Wilcox's place has added largely to our stores having discovered somewhere in town a mine of rum old rum & [*illegible*] we have now a regularly established well organized bar & Henry our nigger is a proficient at the art of cocktails wh are served at first light every morning! After Bk Goree came in and informs us that Genl Longstreet starts today up the Valley & asks me to accompany him. I go off for my horse & found that some other friend of Col Johnstons has her for the day—Genl Longstreet in his thick boots with heavy brass spurs is a noble figure 6 feet & broadshouldered with a most good humored face somewhat ruddy (with exposure & short auburn hair) slightly [*illegible*] altogether a soldier & when he swings himself into his [*illegible*] saddle & set in motion a powerful bay stallion which he rides, with his short military cape over his shoulders he is indeed a type of Athletic Cavalier whose picture Walter Scott has so often recorded—

Varina (Howell) Davis (1826–1906) and her husband. The wife of the Confederate president was "a great talker & very bitter," according to Conolly, and made numerous sneering comments that struck the M.P. as "intolerable." Conolly quickly learned to steer clear of Mrs. Davis, writing that "I went several evenings to pay my respects to Jeff. who commanded my respect but always avoided the tigress." *Virginia Historical Society*

Dinner with same party as before at General Anderson's excellent in every partic. with some very fine Sherry Admiral Buchanan[54] who fought the gallant action in Hampton Roads with the famous Merrimac was there and a finer old naval officer does not exist Genl Anderson is proprietor of the Tredegar iron works here where the shot & shell as well as cannon for the Confed. States are all manufactured I hear a splendid establishment wh I will see—Old Doctor McGill[55] from Hagerstown Maryland 6 feet 2 one of the grenadiers a most cheery soldierlike old fellow full of anecdotes of the war & the fearful fields he has witnessed Spottsylvania Cold Harbour Malvern Hill[56]—

WEDNESDAY, 15 MARCH

Started in camp attire my old leather breeches & jack boots & spurs flannel shirt & brown jacket with a haversack of provisions, pistol & Knife—pipe & a large bag of Tobacco. Met little Capt Ward[57] A.D.C. to Genl Wilcox at Train & in 2 hours arrived at the Dunlop station near Petersburg (24 miles) where Major Taylor provided us with an Ambulance & capital Mules conveyed us thro' the city of Petersburg to Wilcox's camp[58] on arrival dine with staff on Soup & extraordinary hashed beef & corn bread Wilcox comes in providentially with a bottle of claret otherwise these poor fellows have nothing but water—Genl has no better fare served on a plate with very seedy steel Knife & fork in his own tent. After dinner go & see Genl. & Mrs Pryor[59]

[54]Franklin Buchanan (1800–1874) had commanded the CSS *Virginia* (formerly USS *Merrimack*) in her encounter with the USS *Monitor* in 1862 (*ECW*, p. 86).

[55]Maryland physician Charles Macgill (1806–1881) had been imprisoned for his Confederate sympathies. After release, he went to Richmond and served as an army medical officer (John McGill, comp., *The Macgill-McGill Family of Maryland* . . . [Washington, D.C., 1948], pp. 217–19).

[56]These Virginia battles took place on 1 July 1862 (Malvern Hill), 8–21 May 1864 (Spotsylvania), and 1–3 June 1864 (Cold Harbor).

[57]Baltimore lawyer Francis Xavier Ward (d.1914) had been wounded as a member of a mob that attacked a U.S. regiment in his hometown in April 1861. Believing Ward would die of his wounds, a college friend composed the words to "Maryland, My Maryland" as a tribute to a southern martyr (*SHSP*, XXIX, 258; *CV*, XXII [1914], 520).

[58]Wilcox recalled that Conolly "made me three visits in my winter quarters near Petersburg, called to see Gen. Lee, dined with him, and secured one of his photographs. He was greatly delighted when I asked him to ride with me along my skirmish line" (*SHSP*, IV, 22n).

[59]Petersburg lawyer, editor, and congressman Roger Atkinson Pryor (1828–1919) rose to brigadier general in 1862 but later was without a command when his regiments were reassigned. He was captured in 1864 and released shortly before Conolly's visit. In 1848 he had

in a neat farm house[60] close by—Very interesting nice people—Pryor a man of learning & intelligence Lawyer & Newspaper Editor who has travelled much but joined army when war broke out & served as Col. & Brigadier—Was taken by Yanks & 7 months in Fort Warren[61]—Go down to Petersburg on old black horse lately captured from Yanks Wilcox riding his old white charger of many battles pleasant evening at Mrs Meade's[62] singing &c. back ll excellent quarters at Pryor's house where Wilcox insisted on placing me[63]—Very sound sleep

Petersburg city on the Appomattox R. is a very considerable place with large Markets Tobacco factories & handsome streets filled with large stores it was 2 years ago hotly contested for by the two armies[64] & the Yanks failing to get it on the first onset entrenched themselves before it in the position they still hold & for a week shelled the town so that altho the damage has to a great extent been repaired almost every house bears the marks of the Enemys wrath. The Church steeple too has a hole thro' wh the light streams near the top where it was struck but remains erect still. They have for a year & a half discontinued the practice tho' the Railway train rarely comes nearer than Dulop station owing to their taking its arrival as the propitious moment for their amusement. All the houses we visit bore marks of the shelling & the Ladies [tell?] us how miserably they spent that week in the cellars with all the [mattresses?] piled on the floor above to make a bom proof—

Genl Wilcox quarters are about 2 miles beyond Petersburg near a smiling farm house (Pryors) & in a grove of trees & about 2 miles from the extreme right of the Confed. Lines—He is a thoroughly competent West Point officer

---

married Sara Agnes Rice (1830–1912) (*Gray*, pp. 247–48; Robert S. Holzman, *Adapt or Perish: The Life of General Roger A. Pryor, C.S.A.* [Hamden, Conn., 1976]).

[60]The Robert D. McIlwaine house, known as Cottage Farm, southwest of Petersburg.

[61]Fort Warren, in Boston harbor, housed prominent Confederates prisoners. Conolly was wrong, however, about both the duration and place of Pryor's imprisonment. Pryor spent about four months at Fort Lafayette prison in New York (Holzman, *Adapt or Perish*, pp. 76–83).

[62]Possibly the home of Richard Kidder Meade, corner of Perry and Washington Sts.

[63]Mrs. Pryor was less than elated: "Under these circumstances you may imagine my sensation at receiving the following note:—'MY DEAR MRS. PRYOR: General Lee has been honored by a visit from the Hon. Thomas Connolly, Irish M.P. from Donegal. He ventures to request you will have the kindness to give Mr. Connolly a room in your cottage, if this can be done without inconvenience to yourself.' Certainly I could give Mr. Connolly a room; but just as certainly I could not feed him! The messenger . . . hastily reassured me. He had been instructed to say that Mr. Connolly would mess with General Lee" (Mrs. Roger A. Pryor, *My Day: Reminiscences of a Long Life* [New York, 1909], pp. 235–36).

[64]The siege began a year earlier, not two. See Richard J. Sommers, *Richmond Redeemed: The Siege at Petersburg* (Garden City, N.Y., 1981).

of excellent sense & European manner he has commanded most successfully in this war & the battle of Gaines Hill[65] fought entirely by his Division is one of the most brilliant as his account is the most graphic & concise of the whole war.[66]

Thursday, 16 March

Genl R. E. Lee "General in Cheif of the Armies of the Southern Confederacy"[67] Genl commanding the army of Virginia the idol of his soldiers & the Hope of His Country is also the handsomest man in all that constitutes the real dignity of man that I ever saw. a large rich intense blue-ish grey eye a beautifully shaped head, a most benign expression, manly healthful complexion, iron grey beard neatly trimmed, a nose slightly acquiline, a small well shaped mouth, erect with commanding porte & long graceful kneck, solidly embedden in broad manly shoulders & deep chest the whole supported by a lightly knit muscular frame of more than the average height make together with an easy courteous manner one of the most prepossessing figures that ever bore the weight of command or led the fortunes of a Nation. add to this the prestige which surrounds his person & the almost fanatical belief in his judgement & capacity wh is the one idea of an entire people & there stands before you the beau ideal of an accomplished & self reliant cheif directing with a firm hand & sagacious head the mighty machine of war.

We visited him at his quarters a neat farm house with a willow tree in its first spring leaves before the door & apple trees round the gable used for tying up the numerous courier horses, & were ushered into the A.D.C. room & find 5 good-looking gentlemen in neat Confed. grey jackets at work at their returns & correspondence one does the honors & despatches another to apprize the Genl in 2 min. he returns & takes Genl Wilcox & myself at once into the opp. room where Genl Lee rises gracefully from his pine table & welcomes me cordially—half an hour easy conversation & as I excuse myself on acct of his pressing business he asks us to dinner at 3.30—so we

---

[65]Wilcox was at the battle of Gaines' Mill, 27 June 1862, though not in the dominant role Conolly describes. Perhaps he confused some other engagement with this one.

[66]Appendix: "Genl Wilcoxs Divisional order."

[67]Lee was not appointed general of all Confederate armies until early 1865. Appendix: "General R. E. Lee."

Of Robert E. Lee (1807–1870) Conolly wrote after visiting the general at his Petersburg headquarters that he was "the handsomest man in all that constitutes the real dignity of man that I ever saw." *Miley Collection, Virginia Historical Society*

A camp in the Federal army besieging Petersburg, March 1865. On the 16th of that month Conolly toured the Confederate defenses and recorded that within "200 to 500 yds from the pickets of the Enemy, we could see his men on his 1st line quietly moving to & fro & a hugh Yankee ensign waving in the breeze!" *Library of Congress*

mount our horses & away at full galop to the extreme right of the Lines &
passing thro' a battery with guns mounted & all on the alert we take the
line of the dismantled Weldon Ry[68] to the advance pickets about 1 mile in
front of the Lines & from 200 to 500 yds from the pickets of the Enemy, we
could see his men on his 1st line quietly moving to & fro & a huge Yankee
ensign waving in the breeze! Continuing up the line of pickets from the
intersection of the Ry to the extreme right we got a capital idea of the Pickets & the watchfulness of the men one man standing on the top of the
breastwork of each small redoubt while the others lounged or slept inside,
some with remains of a fire some without & all provided with rough shan-
ties to ward off wind & rain These sentinels could be distinguished with
the glass at equal intervals all along the line the small redoubts being about
250 yds apart & occasional officers on duty up & down the pickets while
Major———[69] The accomplished cheif of Sharpshooters was everywhere
from his hut about 100 yds in rear of the pickets & overlooking entire
arrangement. He told the Genl he had marked a house about 600 yds from
the pickets where he had seen several officers meet & 6 or 7 horses were
seen to enter from time to time & proposed to descend upon it next night
with a picked lot of men & capture the entire [*illegible*]—About a mile on
Wilcox showed me the scene of a quick & bloody fight of 3 months ago
where he had in an hour knocked over 500 of the enemy with the loss of
30 men—The ruined farm ho. in the middle of the field showed signs of
shot & musketry & the formation of the Land showed exactly how the Confeds were sheltered while forming the Attack & finally put the aggressive
force to rout—

Genl Heath[70] a most courteous, handsome man galloped us to his quarters
& supplied us with excellent cocktail, find Captain Davis[71] on his staff s. of
Inspector of Cambridge Police—Genl Heath is well appointed & rides a
beautiful black stallion thoroughbred—To dine with Genl Lee. 6 at Table

[68]The Weldon Railway connected Petersburg to North Carolina and had been the scene of
fighting in the summer of 1864 before the siege developed (*ECW*, pp. 812–13).

[69]There are two candidates for this unnamed officer. He could have been Major William
Simpson Dunlop, author of *Lee's Sharpshooters...* (Little Rock, 1899). Or he could have been
Major Thomas J. Wooten, "a terror to the enemy's picket lines," commander, regimental sharp-
shooters, 18th N.C. Regiment (*NCT*, VI, 306, 412).

[70]Henry Heth (1825–1899), major general, C.S.A. (*Gray*, p. 133). His headquarters were at
the Venable/Pickering House on the Boydton Plank Road southwest of Petersburg. Footnote:
"Genl Heath commission to London Capt. Burton Geograph. Soc. London on pt. of Lt. General
Heath—Petersburg Camp."

[71]Footnote: "Captain Davis s. of Cap. Davis Inspector of Cambridgeshire Police—."

(Col. Venable,[72] Genl Wilcox Col. Taylor,[73] T. Conolly Major Venable[74] Genl R. E. Lee) His easy simplicity of conversation with "his boys"—His quiet orderly table & Spartan fare Thick hoch poch soup full of vegetables of wh we all had 2 bowls as Genl says always 2 turns of soup in camp & a third if you like it Mr Conolly he opens himself a flask of very old Madeira wh had been in his old house & had been among the few things saved when his family had to turn out before the Yankee invaders. Excellent! just 2 glasses round The Genl says his simple grace & sits next me letting his boys help—. After soup the dinner consisted of one dish only & accompaniments of excellent rice & vegetables galore, But that dish was a splendid one The largest Turkey I ever saw which fed us all off one side when it was brought in by the single military servant I could not refrain from the exclamation "My eyes what a Turkey"! Yes said the Genl "you are in luck to day Mr Conolly that turkey was the present of a kind Lady in Petersburg & I have kept him 5 days, fattening on soldiers rice He was intended for the President but as he has not come I ordered him for you" He was much interested in my account of the Camp at Chalons[75] & the Emperor of the French & was delighted with Major Venables account of his escape from the Yankees after he had been captured & his romantic marriage & return to the Confederacy!—Venables was Lieutenant of Cavalry under the famous J. E. B Stuart[76] & his men were engaged with the enemy's Cavalry & had driven them into a wood at the other side of which another party of Stuarts Cavalry had been sent round to intercept them Venables was ordered to get to the party by this same circuit & retire them but taking the turn too soon as he thought he could descry the grey confed. uniforms by the morning light thro' the bush he came right into a posse of Yankee cavalry & still believing them to be his own men, chided them for advancing so far & was ordering them to retire when he found himself a Prisoner. He was taken to the Yank army & put with others into the cars for Philadelphia & waiting for dark got his legs out of the window & while

---

[72]Charles Scott Venable (1827–1900). See Jeffry D. Wert, " 'The Tycoon:' Lee and His Staff," *Civil War Times Illustrated*, XI, no. 4 (July 1972), 12–13.

[73]Walter Herron Taylor (1838–1916), an aide to Lee throughout the war (*CV*, XXIV [1916], 174).

[74]Andrew Reid Venable, Jr. (1832–1909), a cavalry officer when captured in October 1864 (*SHSP*, XXXVII, 61–73).

[75]Napoleon III's military camp near Chalons-sur-Marne. Writing "Aux quartiers Imperiales," Conolly informed his sister, "I am here by invitation of the Emperor this morning & find myself in clover.... The Emperor treated me as before with the greatest kindness" (Thomas Conolly to Harriet Conolly, 19 Aug. 1863, Conolly MSS, quoted by permission of the Board of Trinity College Dublin).

[76]For James Ewell Brown Stuart (1833–1864), major general, C.S.A., see Emory M. Thomas, *Bold Dragoon: The Life of J. E. B. Stuart* (New York, 1986).

the train was running full speed gave himself a cant with his elbows & lighted clear of the train on an embankment & tho' sorely bruised managed to get into Philadelphia where he had relatives—He then managed to communicate with a young Lady at St Louis to whom he was engaged & she came down & met him in Baltimore where they were married—She procured a disguise for him & he travelled to Cumberland where he forded the Potomac & got back to his Duty.—Another story followed of a Lad who was engaged to a young Lady at Baltimore taking the oath of allegiance to the Yankee in order to get to his Lady Love—She was overjoyed at first sight of him but when he confessed to her the means by wh he had got thro' she said, all is over Sir between us I beg you to leave my sight for ever!—

FRIDAY, 17 MARCH[77]

After dinner Genl Lee showed me the defences of Richmond on the map extending in a Line of 35 miles from the E of Richmond to 5 miles W of the Appotomax & Petersburg He showed me also the enemies lines confronting them nearly the entire way with each of his bastions & battery (marked & numbered. Now he said we have 2 lines of defence [*illegible*] those shown on this map wh are separate & distinct fortifications capable of being held if such were our Policy for ever! on this momentous Question viz. Whether under certain circumstances the exegencies of the war might not render it advisable to evacuate Richmond I of course said nothing Tho' when pressed by an injudicious young Lady Oh General Lee I hope you'll never give up Richmond He floor'd her by saying *"Oh Miss have you no faith in our boys* He gave me his photograph & Southern flag & we took horse & went to spend "the balance of the evening" at Petersburg at the charming house of Mr Dunlop[78] where we heard Patriotic songs from the young Ladies & many a good story of the war as there were several nice young fellows there—The manners of these fine fellows to the Ladies were very pretty & their reception most cordial! It rained heavily as we went home & it was a difficult path across the fields & thro gullys but Genl Wilcox piloted the way (pitch dark) & we got home wind blowing half a gale & the tent fluttering & shaking like a bad umberella—I had again my comfortable lodging at Genl Pryors & we were asked to breakfast next day by dear Mrs Pryor one of the nicest Ladies I ever saw.[79]

[77]Note beside the date: "Patrick's Day." From the text it is apparent that he put the date in the wrong place.

[78]Possibly Robert Dunlop, tobacco manufacturer, whose house was at Lombard and Fourth Sts.

[79]The date, Friday, 17 March 1865, should have been placed here.

The Major Allen with whom Conolly shared an extravagant breakfast on 20 March was probably Major William Griffin Orgain Allen (1815–1875), of Claremont Manor in Surry County. Allen, like Conolly, was a great patron of the turf and, according to another chronicler of wartime Richmond, "was unhappily overindulgent to his own tastes for the best solids and fluids. He made money flow like water, and all bibulents flow like the money." *Virginia Historical Society*

Capital Bk & smoke & then to horse & down to the Station beyond Petersburg "Dunlop Depot" where I met Venables & travelled with him to Richmond. Crossing the James by a very high bridge without any battlement nearly 1/4 of a mile dizzy crossing! Arrived in time for Table d'hote & visited Mrs Capt Ward in the Evening! She takes me out to an Evg Party at Mrs Doswells & I have the satisfaction of telling her how admirably Papa Doswell was dancing the Virginia Reel (our Sir Roger de Coverley) at Mrs Lafittes[80] at Nassau—Pleasant Evg—Bed at 11.

SATURDAY, 18 MARCH

Find Portman & Kirkham back again having met with some of Sherman's raiders near Piping tree Ferry[81] & been robbed of their watches &c. They were camping out when the raiders came on them asleep & with pistols to their heads made them shell-out—They returned with much anxiety as to other raiders & very glad to get back! Portman[82] reinstalled in his bed in our room—Go to visit Col Lay[83] in return for his [kd?] offer of his buggy & hear Miss Carey[84] & Miss Campbell sing—Dine & go to Genl Andersons to tea— walk with Mrs Booth

SUNDAY, 19 MARCH

To Church with little girls[85] To see Genl Lees family after church Dine at Hotel with old party & walk in Franklin St with Ladies—Tea &c. write some poetry for Mrs Helm[86] & write up Log

---

[80]The wife of Jean Baptiste Lafitte, an agent at Nassau for John Fraser and Company of Charleston, a shipping firm controlled by George Alfred Trenholm, Confederate secretary of the treasury (Wise, *Lifeline*, chap. 2).

[81]Piping Tree, on the Pamunkey River 20 miles northeast of Richmond, "is not remarkable for any thing more than a comfortable tavern house and ferry" (Joseph Martin, *New and Comprehensive Gazetteer of Virginia . . .* [Charlottesville, 1836], p. 205). Perhaps Conolly thought of all northern cavalrymen as "Sherman's raiders," or perhaps he just confused Sherman with Sheridan, whose troops did pass through nearby King William County on 17–19 March.

[82]Footnote: "see signatures."

[83]Appendix: "Col Lays letter—voir No26." Col. George W. Lay, on Gen. Joseph E. Johnston's staff in 1861 and later chief of the Bureau of Conscription (*SHSP*, XXX, 51).

[84]Possibly Constance (Cary) Harrison (1843–1920), one of the belles of wartime society in Richmond.

[85]Footnote: "See Signatures of my angels." Signatures at back of diary: Sarah Lee Simpson and Sallie Richer Harwood, of Petersburg, and Ella Steele Montgomery, of Montgomery, Ala.

[86]Appendix: "Helms dirge." Conolly's poem is in the scrapbook of mementoes of his trip.

Monday, 20 March

Up & Bk 8.30 with Col. Sutherland[87] at Major Allen's[88] Fine old Virginia family great planter on the James & owner of 600 negroes before the war—very pleasant & breakfast exuberant in Virginia delicacies of different sorts of hot bread, Meat fish, Eggs &c cocktails & cigar meet an Irish gardener from Castle Coole[89] one Boone, came up with the President & enjoy a short chat with him! Walk with Mrs Brown out shopping!—Dinner at Uncle Tom Griffins[90] Mrs Brown, Mrs Booth, Miss Hearndon[91] Portman Sterrett Stringer,[92] Col. Sutherland, Tom Snead & self very good dinner but vy bad wine—Evening at Presidents, Miss Maggie Howell very nice Mrs Davis eloquent against Seward[93] & yankee nation—But bitter malevolent tongue, very unamiable

Tuesday, 21 March

Find Col Lays buggy & nice pair of horses at the door & prevail on Mrs Brown to go to the Revue of Longstreets Div: Pleasant day & most interesting revue all the Ladies of Richmond. Miss Thomas[94] the Bell—little McCann[95]

[87]Possibly Lt. Col. S. F. Sutherland of the 3rd Infantry Regiment Local Defense Troops (Departmental) (*CMH*, III, 560).

[88]Probably Maj. William Griffin Orgain Allen (1815–1875) of Claremont Manor in Surry County on the James. He reputedly owned 30,000 acres and 800 slaves before the war (Mary A. Stephenson, *Old Homes in Surry & Sussex* [Richmond, 1942], pp. 30–31). Allen would have been the perfect boon companion for Conolly. He "was a great horseman, hunter and sailor; had a craze for rare stock and pits, was unhappily overindulgent to his own tastes for the best solids and fluids. He made money flow like water, and all bibulents flow like the money" (T. C. De Leon, *Belles Beaux and Brains of the 60's* [New York, 1907], p. 133).

[89]Seat of the earl of Belmore, near Enniskillen, Co. Fermanagh.

[90]An account of social life in wartime Richmond referred to the excellent meals served by "old Tom Griffin" (De Leon, *Belles*, p. 401).

[91]Possibly either Lucy or Molly Herndon, daughters of a Confederate naval doctor and prominent in the social life of the wartime capital. They were friends of the Enders family, who were among Conolly's acquaintants (ibid., p. 151). See entry for 1 April.

[92]Conolly first met Stringer in Raleigh, North Carolina, on 6 March.

[93]Unknown to Conolly, U.S. Secretary of State William Henry Seward (1801–1872) had received several dispatches about the M.P.'s trip to the South.

[94]A signature in the diary, "Willie Thomas Miss Nannie Thomas' brother Fairfax Va.," and the 1850 census (p. 133), suggest that she was the daughter of Julia M. (Jackson) Thomas and Henry Wirtz Thomas (1812–1890). Her father, a longtime resident of Fairfax County, served in the Confederate Senate and moved his family to Richmond during the war. In 1872 Nannie (1844–1890) married Benjamin Eglin (or Elgin) (1838–1914) (George Wesley Rogers, *Officers of the Senate of Virginia, 1776–1956* [Richmond, 1959], pp. 55–56; marriage and death certificates, Fairfax, Virginia, circuit court archives and city cemetery records).

[95]Identified at back of diary as "Capt. Charles McCann commanding Scouts Gearys Brigade Born at Old Castle near Trillick County Tyrone Ireland. Citizen of Petersburg Va."

the scout officer (islander) Genls Geary[96] Breckenridge[97] Longstreet Fitz-hugh Lee[98] &c &c &c &. back for dinner wet Evening—Visit from sagacious old Doctor MacGill formerly a Revolutionary Leader at Baltimore now convert & anti-Democracy man—His stories & [*illegible*] Experiences in the war "Leg & Boot Story" Spotsylvania McCann tells Sterrett of the dangers of the route to Maryland.

Wednesday, 22 March

Up at 5.30 Sterrett & dear Mrs Brown go "away' to try the Fredericksburg route for New York[99]—read & write up—Get 50 from Bank of Branch[100] where I was introduced by invaluable Sterrett. Pay $1930 dollars Confed. money for dinner on Monday—and 9000 for Pictures of the crater at Petersburg & the Scout: 1000 for Hotel expenses.[101] Drive with little Stringer at Congress hall. Smoke cocktail & Walk with Mrs Booth.

Thursday, 23 March

Take Mrs Booth & Willy[102] to be photographed to see Col Johnston & rest at Office of Pres:[103] go with Burwell to see Col Branch[104] in Broad St smoke

[96]Martin Witherspoon Gary (1831–1881), brigadier general, C.S.A., commander of the last Confederate forces to leave Richmond (*Gray*, p. 102). See entry for 9 May.

[97]John Cabell Breckinridge (1821–1875), former U.S. vice-president, presidential candidate in 1860, major general, C.S.A., and last Confederate secretary of war (*DAB*, III, 7–10)

[98]Fitzhugh Lee (1835–1905), nephew of R. E. Lee and major general, C.S.A. (*Gray*, pp. 178–79).

[99]See entry for 22 April.

[100]Branch Morton & Co. recorded on this day, with "Hon. Thos. Conolly," a "Sale 50£ Stg His own Bill on Lewis Harris Dublin," for which the M.P. received $13,333.33. Conolly added in the margin the figures given below for a total of $11,900; not surprisingly, he was back for more on 23 March and 1 April (Cash Book 1865, Branch & Co., Richmond, Va., Records, VHS).

[101]The creator of these popular prints was John Adams Elder (1833–1895). See Margaret Coons, "A Portrait of His Times: John Elder's Paintings . . . ," *Virginia Cavalcade*, XVI (Spring 1967), 15–31.

[102]Conolly met Mrs. Booth and Willy again, on 22 April, in New York City, where they apparently lived but gave no explanation why they were in Richmond.

[103]Marginal note: "Get letter &c from Capt Lee at the Marine for going down to see Adl Semmes on Saturday—Write to Wilcox for Monday—!!!"

[104]Probably Thomas Branch, a leading commission merchant of Petersburg and Richmond (*OB*, No. 49 [Dec. 1984], 1–5).

with him & Dr Patterson[105] till Ladies come home from [*illegible*] pleasant Evg—

FRIDAY, 24 MARCH

Get Col. Johnstons horse & out to Longstreets Division See the Staff Latrobe[106] Fairfax,[107] Goree, Alexander[108] go on with Goree to Genl Geary's division of Cavalry & find my friend McCann with whom we dine on bacon & beans & indian meal—! Geary is a right damn good fellow—! & a hard 'un—McCann comes with me into Richmond across the fields & ravines See the 2nd and 3rd Lines of Defences he tells me that they apprehend a fight on Extreme left & have been warned tonight to take pickets & try [conclusions?]! Grant has moved 1 Division from S of the James to N. & they expect an attack take a drink & smoke & then to & pass the evening with the beautiful & accomplished Miss Thomas the belle of Richmond she tells us of her being imprisoned & searched & her brave conduct He told me I was the greatest rebel he had met. I would have told you "you are the greatest altho the prettiest rebel I ever saw."[109]

Smoke with Stringer & hear the band & run down to see 3,000 men pass from Petersburg to the left in accordance with McCanns' information—!!

Bed. &c—sleep till 9 very tired!

[105]Possibly R. M. Patterson, in 1864 an assistant surgeon, General Hospital No. 21, Cary and 25th Sts. (Wyndham B. Blanton, *Medicine in Virginia in the Nineteenth Century* [Richmond, 1933], p. 304n.

[106]Osmun Latrobe (1835–1915), appointed to Longstreet as adjutant general in late 1864, kept a diary between 1862 and 1865, a copy of which is at the Virginia Historical Society. Unfortunately he made no mention of Conolly.

[107]John Walter Fairfax (1828–1908), aide to Longstreet (Lyon G. Tyler, ed., *Men of Mark in Virginia* . . . [Washington, D.C., 1908], IV, 115–18).

[108]William Kirkwood Alexander (b.1846), a VMI cadet at New Market and on Longstreet's staff (William Couper, *The V.M.I. New Market Cadets* [Charlottesville, 1933], p. 11).

[109]Footnote: "Miss Thomas when her Fathers house was invaded by the Yankees was asked by the Officer who was in the house she replied my Mother & myself, Where is your brother Where he ought to be Sir! Where is he With Genl Lee Sir! Where is your Sweetheart In Genl Lees army or nowhere Madame There is a paper for you to sign here is a pen I should like to read it Sir first Oh it is a mere form—What Sir it a declaration of allegiance—Certainly Madam Well I shall not sign Madam I am sorry but you will have to go to Prison if you dont Well Sir You may take me to Prison & to Prison she went & was there separated from her mother for 10 days, & then put into an ambulance & sent back home!"

CHAPTER THREE

"A FANCIED INVINCIBILITY"

SATURDAY, 25 MARCH

Bk in my room far better than in the public room.! Everything arranged for Wilcox & the Camp on Monday 1 Turkey 1 ham half a dozen of whiskey & two bags of Zarvona[1] tobacco as stores Henry (The boy) added 2 doz hard cooked eggs! All Right Henry! you may go [*illegible*] Down to Stringers & with him to Capt Ley[2] at the [Marine?] to prepare for our expedition down the River to see Semmes Adl Semmes of the "Alabama" & "Sumpter" Semmes! Semmes! We are handed over to Lieut. Roberts[3] of the "Torpedo" gun boat wh Capt Ley had kindly placed at my disposal to convey us down the River "Jeames" to the fleet below Drewry's Bluff Fortifications[4]—

Walk down with him & Stringer to the wharf where we find "The Torpedo" with steam up & go swinging down the beautiful beer-colored Jeames passing all the stake obstructions & two bridges of wood light triangle form[5] till we get to the last obstructions where a regular fortification has been made by sinking crates of stones & whole steamers with only their top paddles & [*illegible*] engine like grim spectres protruding above the plashing waves & a narrow passage only known to the mysterious between the stakes

[1]Probably named for Richard Thomas (1833–1875), a dropout from the U.S. Military Academy who in Asia fought Chinese pirates, in Europe changed his name to Zarvona when campaigning with Garibaldi, and in America became a Confederate hero when, disguised as a female passenger, he captured a Baltimore steamer (Charles A. Earp, "The Amazing Colonel Zarvona," *MHM*, XXXIV [1939], 334–43).

[2]According to a letter from Col. George W. Lay, in Conolly's scrapbook, "Capt. Ley" was the same "Capt. Lee" mentioned on 27 March and was Sidney Smith Lee (1802–1869), brother of R. E. Lee.

[3]Appendix: "Lieut Roberts of the 'Torpedo' Semmes fleet of ironclads."

[4]The defences at Drewry's Bluff were on the James River about 7 miles downstream from Richmond.

[5]At this point Conolly drew a sketch of the bridge.

Conolly visited the diminutive fleet of Confederate Admiral Raphael Semmes
(1809–1877) at Drewry's Bluff, Virginia, on 25 March. Despite what he told
Conolly, Semmes was hardly sanguine about the Confederacy's prospects.
When he arrived at Drewry's Bluff he "soon had the mortification to find that
the fleet was as much demoralized as the army." *Virginia Historical Society*

at the side. *slow* & round & then thro! grazing the stakes & then full swing
again down to the fleet with the Southern cross flying & funnels smoking
bristling with cannon & men like bees all on & round the 3 huge Monitors &
attendant "Gun boats" salute Admiral's flag & swing past & bring up finding
him walking the deck of his Monitor "Virginia"[6] looking as hard & determined as flint with his pointed moustache & well weather-beaten thin cut
face He was surrounded by his officers & received us kindly walking us
across a single balk of timbers wh protruded from her side with similar balks
all around her to prevent Torpedo boats approach, a pleasant visit sometimes hard in these quarters as Lieut. Roberts more fully explained in the
case of his ship the Albemarle[7] wh was lying at Plymouth when one dark
night Lieut. Cushing U.S.N. came quietly in his steam launch & ran his Torpedo under her & then jumping into the water swam to shore where he lay
for 24 hours in the sedge till night again favoring him he cut loose a canoo &
rowed himself safely thro' the whole fleet back to his Flag-ship meantime the
Albemarle went slowly & gracefully to the bottom & thence to Hell—Capt.
Clapell[8] then a Lieut tried to pay the same compliment to the gigantic Yankee "Ironsides" & was capture in the water after the attempt & when the
stoker gallantly sticking by the Launch backed her during the confusion &
got back safely to Charleston!—

[*Illegible*] Admiral Semmes conducted us across his bridge namely the
aforesaid balk of timber with a hand line of ropes suspended between the
"awful Virginia"[9] & a large barge alongside constituted pro. tem. his office
into wh we descended Down a ladder backwards & found his paraphernalia
of pistols, sabres, boarding pikes compass. inkstand & writing book with a
pidgeon hole shelf of dockets in due order & a sickly boy "My son sir" who
has been bad with diarrhoha all in their places & take a seat Sir & Capt Dunnington[10] my flag Capt &c when we sat down & I produced my credentials a
letter from old Portman & enquiries after him, & then same after Stringers[11]
family & then general conversation till Semmes suggested you wd like to see
the Monitor Capt D. led the way thro a small iron port hole where we saw
the thickness of her iron-sides lined with oak about 4 feet when inside the

[6]CSS *Virginia II.*

[7]William B. Cushing commanded the torpedo boat that sank the CSS *Albemarle* on 27 October 1864 (*ECW*, p. 5).

[8]Appendix (same as five notes above): "Lieut Roberts of the 'Torpedo' Semmes fleet of iron-clads."

[9]Footnote: "List of Monitors &c & commanders."

[10]John W. Dunnington, lieutenant commanding the CSS *Virginia II*, had earlier com-manded the CSS *Owl* (*ORN*, ser. ii, II, 765–67).

[11]See entry for 6 March when Conolly first met Stringer.

great guns one astern of gigantic proportion do for'ad & 3 at either side light & air coming thro thick iron bars at top, sides sloping inwards garnished with all the gun requisites tower tier filled with long steel soled shot about 12 inches each. middle supports covered with racks of six & ten shooting rifles in fine order men & officers sauntering about quietly—Thence to mens quarters down a hatchway for'ad all in order with a cooking stove full of excellent dinner surrounded by mess boxes wh when opened had their tin plates, cups knives salt pepper &c in good array with the no of rations for each mess in middle! All as nice as any man of war hammocks all stowed along inside making a pleasant couch to lean against—Men all standing round at attention & all neatly clad in confed: grey shirts Then to engine room at other end—Thro. wardroom & quarters Adls sleeping room all dark but bright & clean when lighted up. Back again to Adls Office in the barge after having a long talk with officers in Ward Room wh was headed by Semmes declaring he could not hope for any Intervention but was sure the Confederacy could & would fight it out to a success![12]

Back again to Richmond its Spires & white pillared capitol shining above the haze & Roofs in the setting sun Richmond thy Sun is not setting rather the Day is just about to break over your hero-crested virgin hills! Always darkest before the dawn! What a dawn Independence!—Find[13] a letter from Mr Ambler Mrs Masons son in law inviting me to dinner at 5 & *"Llewellyn Saundersons"*[14] name on my table are cheerful notes! To Mrs Mason's dear old Mrs Mason & hear that "Welly" is to be there 3 Miss Masons Major Mason Genl. Custis Lee[15] Welly Miss [Clerk?] T. Conolly Col. Brown[16] of Ordnance Dept Mr Ambler & 2 more Mrs Mason at the head of her genial table of modest plenty!!! & Welly comes in with a History of adventure parallel to mine

[12]Semmes was not so sanguine. Arriving at Drewry's Bluff, he "soon had the mortification to find that the fleet was as much demoralized as the army. . . . Great discontent and restlessness prevailed" (Raphael Semmes, *Memoirs of Service Afloat* . . . [Baltimore, 1869], p. 803).

[13]Appendix: "Amblers letter [*illegible*]." In 1847 John Ambler (b.1821) had married Anna Mason (1826–1863). See entry for 8 March.

[14]Llewellyn Traherne Bassett Saunderson (b.1841), of Dromkeen House, County Cavan, reached the Chesapeake Bay from Nova Scotia on 17 March. He was an aide to Gen. Fitzhugh Lee during the retreat from Petersburg (*OR*, ser. i, XLVI, pt. i, 1305; Burke's *Landed Gentry* [1879], p. 1419). His brief memoir of these experiences is, like Conolly's, owned by the Castletown Foundation, and a copy is at the VHS.

[15]George Washington Custis Lee (1832–1913), eldest son of R. E. Lee, aide to Jefferson Davis, and major general, C.S.A. (*Gray*, p. 179).

[16]Possibly John Willcox Brown (b.1833), forced by illness to leave active service in 1863 for an appointment in the Ordnance Department at Richmond (*CMH*, III, 767–68; Dew, *Ironmaker*, p. 275) or possibly William Leroy Broun (1827–1902), commander of the Richmond arsenal (*CV*, X, 225).

he having come in a schooner from Halifax having vainly tried Bermuda & landed at Gwyenns Island from the Chesapeake & lastly having fallen into the hands of Custis Lees pickets who forwarded him after 12 hours detention in an ambulance So here he is merry & fresh & genial & hearty as ever My dear Welly give us your hand how the devil did you get here!—Mr Ambler does the hosts part most effectively & washes down Mrs Masons profusion of honest plain cookery with excellent brandy & water the only thing now drinkable in Richmond Welly recounts his adventures & we all are happy as larks a small victory on the right near to Petersburg[17] Prisoners came in same evening & were remarked to be almost all drunk![18]

SUNDAY, 26 MARCH

Up at 8 Bk at 9 Daniel produces delicacies poached eggs &c &c Mr Mason[19] comes to talk about Florida Cotton 1,000 Bales—near St. Marks[20] open to an offer—

To the Exchange Hotel[21] for Miss Thomas "the beautiful Rebel" to Ch. with her St Pauls Dr Minnegeode's[22] argument about Man created in the Divine image redeemed back to it sent me to sleep I hate argument I like Faith much better! Back to Exchange & introduced to Mama Thomas & children to walk with la belle at 5 when she tells me as we go thro the faire crowd in Franklin St of her Prison experiences her Tournament with Yankee Brigadier Genl in wh she overthrew the enemy at all points. *Oh you rare girl* Dine with Colonel Preston Johnston & his very nice wife the excellent homely fare & hearty welcome with a glass of toddy & a smoke! Mrs Johnston is about going to Kentucky to sell the remains of her husbands property for anything it will fetch & then take her children to Orleans France where she has a sister & they are going to stay over the crisis of their countrys & her

---

[17]Appendix: "Petersburg success Sat. Mar. 25th 1865."

[18]Footnote: "Tea at Mrs. Stannard her agreeable reminiscences of England, Apsley Ho. [Elvaston?] Ly. Harrington &c. &c. She was astonished to find a cousin of the D of W here!!!" She was probably Judge Robert C. Stanard's wife, whose salons were a highlight of wartime society (Thomas, *Richmond*, p. 116). Conolly was a distant cousin by marriage of the first duke of Wellington, whose London home was Apsley House.

[19]Probably a relative of Mrs. James Murray Mason, though not her husband, who was in London.

[20]On the St. Marks River near the Gulf of Mexico, about 20 miles south of Tallahassee.

[21]On Fourteenth St., a block southeast of Capitol Square.

[22]The Rev. Dr. Charles M. Minnigerode (1814–1894), whose tenure at St. Paul's spanned the years from 1856 to 1889.

On hearing a sermon at St. Paul's Church in Richmond by Dr. Charles Minnigerode (1814–1894), Conolly wrote that it "sent me to sleep I hate argument I like Faith much better!" *Virginia Historical Society*

husbands fate! Everybody has made similar sacrifices & they cry still extermination but no submission!!!!

MONDAY, 27 MARCH[23]

Left Richmond by train at 9 a.m having written to Welly Saunderson, & Miss Thomas also to Capt Lee to prepare for our Expedition to Drury's Bluff

[23]The entries for 27, 28, and 29 March were written on a sheet not bound in the diary.

on Friday—Arrived at Dunlop Station & while waiting there for Genl Wilcox's ambulance to carry self & box of provisions to Camp find hospitable reception with the Station Master of the Georgian Troops Capt Daniel. While there make the acquaintance of Dr Daubeny[24] author of the Life of Stonewall Jackson published by Nisbet & Co. Berners St. London.! a number of Yankee prisoners 150 come up under guard & getting into conversation with them I find one half of them Irish & one John Tobin nephew of Peter Judge of Celbridge[25] who at once recognized me.! Major Adams lends me a horse & I accompany him to Petersburg & find his mess all seedy & Col Wilson an enormous, burly, jolly fellow & 5 others with whom I lunch off excellent [pig face?] & beans followed by Molasses pudding & a good drink of whiskey—Thence to Wilcox & find him suffering from a severe boil under the arm to Tea with Genl & Mrs Pryor & after a pleasant Evg with them find my comfortable room all ready as before.

TUESDAY, 28 MARCH[26]

Up 6—Bk with Pryors at 8. & on horseback to the scene of the battle of Saturday[27] all explained fully by Pryor. only a reconnaissance in force by Genl Lee & so far a brilliant affair tho a considerable loss in [*illegible*] Ransoms' brigade suffered most 700 Bushrod Johnstons[28] 350. on to Genl Heaths see Capt Davis & another staff officer. Heath meets me on the Road & shortly after Mrs Heath & her little daughter in an ambulance They ask me to dine tomorrow! Thence by Wilcox's to Petersburg where [I see?] Mrs Meade & her daughters. Mr Johnston[29] tobacco merchant who extends hospitable cocktails & asks me to Bk next day—Capt Swan from Londonderry also Dr.

[24]Robert Lewis Dabney (1820–1898), a Presbyterian theologian who wrote *Life of Lieut.-Gen. Thomas J. Jackson (Stonewall Jackson)* (London, 1864). Perhaps Conolly mentioned Berners Street because it was only a short walk from his house on Hanover Square.

[25]Peter Judge was a grocer in Celbridge, County Kildare, the village near Castletown.

[26]On this day William Barksdale Myers (1839–1873), wrote from the Petersburg defences to his father, Richmond attorney Gustavus Adolphus Myers, whom Conolly may have visited on 11 March: "what about Connolly, M.P. I hear he has been here but I have never received any notice of that fact—[De?] Leon mentions that he purchased two pictures (Crater and Scout)." (See entry for 22 March.) De Leon possibly was Thomas Cooper De Leon (1839–1914), author of *Belles, Beaux and Brains of the 60's*. Myers continued: "If Mr. Connolly does come here and you likes him, I can show him around the lines, which are not cast in pleasant places and smell" (William Barksdale Myers to Gustavus Adolphus Myers, 28 Mar. 1865, Myers Family Papers, VHS).

[27]The battle of Fort Stedman (*Almanac*, pp. 656–57).

[28]Bushrod Rust Johnston (1817–1880), major general, C.S.A. (*Gray*, pp. 157–58).

[29]Possibly William R. Johnson, whose tobacco factory was at the corner of High and Cross Sts. and whose house was at South End Heights.

Sara Agnes (Rice) Pryor (1830–1912) at first resented
being asked by General Lee to provide a room for Conolly
during his visit to Petersburg. The M.P.'s charms won her
over, however, and she remembered him as "a most agreeable guest, a fine-looking Irish gentleman with an irresistibly humorous, cheery fund of talk." *Virginia Historical Society*

O'Hagan[30] from L. Derry—Back to dine with the staff [*illegible*] comes in
very well especially the Turkey wh. is excellent!! Another whiskey!! out to
see Genl Lee alone, sit with him for an hour most genial kind man, his

[30]Dr. Charles J. O'Hagan, surgeon with Ransom's 9th N.C. Volunteers in 1861 and with Ransom's Brigade at Appomattox (*OR*, ser. i, V, 446; *SHSP*, XV, 424).

Roger Atkinson Pryor (1828–1919), a lawyer, editor, and
congressman from Petersburg, had been a Confederate general but later was without command when his regiments
were reassigned. Captured late in 1864, he had returned
from a northern prison camp only days before Conolly
arrived at the Pryor home in Petersburg. *Virginia Historical
Society*

description of Genl Winfield Scott[31] his egotism but sterling qualities, good
sense, & moderation as shown first on the board at West Point & afterwards
in the Mexican Campaign. Recommends me to read Scotts Life by himself!

[31]Winfield Scott (1786–1866) commanded the U.S. Army in 1861 but, unlike fellow Virginian Col. R. E. Lee, refused to join the Confederate army.

Mrs Lee has it at Richmond![32] Mrs Stannard! & then the devout hopes that his country may have the reward of their Constancy & Virtue!—I join him in this ardent wish & wring his hand—He signs the Confed. Flag for me—[33] Back to Tea with dear Mrs Pryor & the jolly boys[34]—To the tower where little Theo Pryor is studying the [*illegible*] just at [*illegible*] speech "To conquer or die"—There is one of the finest boys I ever saw & is very forward in Mathematics & Geometry—Mrs Pryor makes me a miniature Battle Flag Confederate[35] out of the Bunting of the original Confederate flag first hoisted at Montgomery Alabama in 1861—Good night 10 o'clock—Pryor gives me Stonewall[36] Jackson's sig.

WEDNESDAY, 29 MARCH

Up 6. to Bk at Petersburg with Mr Johnston Excellent Bk meet Genl. Gordon![37] & see two fine young fellows brothers who had been wounded in the battle of Sat. Major & Capt Graham[38] 1st. severely thro both legs—They are kindly attended by Mrs Johnston in her own bed-room[39]—Promise to go & see these gallant fellows again they are as merry as cockchafers!—Back to Wilcox. Order comes in to have his Division ready to join Heath this Evening mix a

[32]On the same day Lee had written his wife, in Richmond, that he was sending her a copy of Scott's *Memoirs of Lieut.-General Scott, LL.D.* (2 vols.; New York, 1864) (Robert E. Lee to Mary Anna Randolph [Custis] Lee, 28 Mar. 1865, Lee Family Papers, VHS).

[33]Footnote: "Genl. Lee explains how slavery was not the object of the war! Virginia first agreed not to secede but entered the movement when Lincoln demanded that it was to be put down by force—"

[34]Mrs. Pryor recalled that "Mr. Conolly interested himself in my boys' Latin studies. 'I am going home,' he said, 'and tell the English women what I have seen here: two boys reading Caesar while the shells are thundering, and their mother looking on without fear.' 'I am too busy keeping the wolf from my door,' I told him, 'to concern myself with the thunderbolts'" (Pryor, *My Day*, pp. 236–37). She had had difficulty obtaining books for her precocious son Theodorick (Holzman, *Adapt or Die*, p. 75).

[35]At this point Conolly drew a small Confederate flag in the text and wrote a footnote: "Mrs Pryors Flag Jewel case with Confed. Flag of R. E. Lee—"

[36]Footnote: "Stonewall Jacksons signature."

[37]John Brown Gordon (1832–1904), major general, C.S.A., had led the unsuccessful attack—Conolly's "battle of Sat."—on Fort Stedman, the failure of which made withdrawal of Petersburg and Richmond imminent (*Gray*, p. 111; *Almanac*, pp. 656–57).

[38]North Carolina Confederate Senator William A. Graham wrote on 26 March, "I received last night a telegram from my son James, informing that his brothers John & Rob't were both wounded—the former in both legs—the latter in the left, in an attack by Gen'l Lee . . . yesterday morning" (Max R. Williams, ed., *The Papers of William Alexander Graham*, Volume VI: *1864–1865* [Raleigh, 1976], p. 289). The major was John Washington Graham (1838–1928), paroled from a Petersburg hospital on 6 May (*LC*, p. 148).

[39]Footnote: "Return of wounded officers Ransoms Brigade."

cocktail for Heaths A.D.C. Capt Selden!!![40] smoke & write in Genl Wilcox tent & discuss tactics till it is time to mount old Grant & gallop over to Genl Heaths to dinner all agog about orders for tomorrow set down 8 at the narrow deal table on forms with tin mugs—excellent soup—pigs head & beans rice & toddy—There were 2 of Ropers[41] men privates who had been at school with Heath very good fellows of the best blood of Virginia but travel stained & harness as well as horses showing the wear of war These fellows were well armed with best Yankee weapons—Genl McGowan[42] Capt Selden Capt Davis[43] (Cambridgeshire) Genl Walker[44] artillery, Genl Heath 2 small men who carved & Thomas Conolly—All went to their duty after dinner while I listened to talk to couriers & passers by—a wounded officer brought in hit near Burgess' mill[45] where Yankees are reported in force! Light a cigar & back to Pryors, Tea & game of whist wh was interrupted by the most terrific bombardment of cannon & shells lighting up the entire line of the enemy for 4 miles & thickest opp: Petersburg we sat at the window wondering, & admiring the effect till 11.30 when it subsided & we went to bed not knowing what to think of it—Excellent sleep—thanks to the Pryors![46]

THURSDAY, 30 MARCH[47]

Wilcox left at 4 I up at 6 to Genl Lees to Bk on old Grant, ford the branch easily & up to Mr Turnbulls[48] to find the General had left for Burgess' Mill at

[40]Considering the exclamation points, this may have been W. Allen Selden, Conolly's fellow passenger on the *Owl*.

[41]Possibly Conolly meant Thomas Lafayette Rosser (1836–1910), major general, C.S.A., present at Petersburg just before the retreat to Appomattox (*Gray*, pp. 264–65).

[42]Samuel McGowan (1819–1897), brigadier general, C.S.A. (ibid, pp. 201–2).

[43]Footnote: "Spencer Rifle with 7 cartridges."

[44]Reuben Lindsay Walker (1827–1890), brigadier general of artillery, C.S.A. (*Gray*, pp. 322–23)

[45]Burgess's Mill was about 12 miles southwest of Petersburg.

[46]Footnote: "Poor Mrs Pryor with her hands clasped Oh how terrible Pryor wandering about tremendous attack you may be sure! This is the Grand final scene! &c &c The rest not knowing anything looking stupidly at the display of fire & listening in silence to the fearful thunderclaps of the artillery the boys outside saying oh how grand &c, &c."

[47]Conolly visited Lee during the last desperate skirmishing before the final Federal assault on the Confederate defences at Petersburg (*Almanac*, pp. 659–61).

[48]At the back of the diary Conolly painted several watercolor sketches, one of which is labeled "Edgehill—the property of J. Turnbull Esq. General R. E. Lee's head-quarters near Petersburg Va—"

3 having according to his habit taken his Bk before starting received kindly by A.D.C. Col. Marshall[49] & old Turnbull—

Very wet morning & getting darker! Bk at 7.30 very plain & good old Turnbull, Marshall & I rest all gone with Genl Lee! Very thick rain in the midst of which I start with Major Cooks A.D.C.[50] for the Field!! 10 miles off toiling thro deep red mud, incessant rain till after an hour we came up with ambulances bearing the names of Corps d'armée & trains of mules roped together & sutlers wagons showing that their army was in front, then crowds of niggers with deserted huts & all the remains of last nights biovuack, couriers on jaded horses spurring thro' the motley collection & we threaded our way to the South side railway & finding an officer in charge there were apprized that Genl Andersons & Ransoms Brigades had passed to the front 2 hours before follow the plank road and thro' the forest till (still raining) we come up to knots of artillery horses picketted their guns being in position & then the works manned & the fires lighted behind them & the soldiers drying their clothes, fires piled up of fir branches tier over tier just like old kitchen ranges & men in every conceivable attitude drying themselves & expending their damp charges & loading again.—Officers on good horses & couriers on ragged jades hurry hither & thither but the line of entrenchments well manned To our enquiries for Genl Lee everybody ready to answer "about a mile ahead near the white oak road" arrive at Burgess's mill now historic[51] & pass the plank bridge, more artillery more men more officers same enquiries, every soldier seemed to know where Genl Lee was 2 miles more of this work thro' roads & shrubs & pools of water all bearing traces of advancing army when at last an open space in the forest (& the musketry begins to ring about a quarter of a mile before us) we come upon the whole staff of the army Genls Pickett, Ransom, Anderson, Heath, Pemberton[52] & old Lee in black mackintosh with his steeple white hat &

[49]Charles Marshall (1830–1902), a grand-nephew of Chief Justice John Marshall, joined Lee's staff in 1862 (Wert, "Lee and His Staff," p. 13).

[50]In his diary on 30 March, Major Giles B. Cooke (1838–1937), of Lee's staff, wrote: "Left for the right with John Cocke about 7:30 A. M. calling by H'dQr's. Met there Mr. Conneley, an English gentleman who came over to this country to see what could be seen. Rode with him to the battlefield.... Had a long and interesting conversation with Mr. Conneley whilst riding down to report to the General. Mr. C. remained with us on the battlefield all day.... The General, Mr. Conneley, Walter Taylor and I left the battlefield about 6 P. M." The skirmishing that so impressed Conolly had become routine to Cooke, who wrote that "we had no fighting of any consequence to-day" (diary of Major Giles B. Cooke, 30 Mar. 1865, VHS).

[51]The mill had become historic because of a fierce battle the previous year.

[52]Confederate generals George Edward Pickett (1825–1875), Matt Whitaker Ransom (1826–1904), and Richard Heron Anderson (1821–1879) (*Gray*, pp. 239–40, 253, 8–9). Although Conolly had met John Clifford Pemberton (1814–1881) before, on 4 March, that

Conolly painted a watercolor sketch at the back of his diary labeled "Edgehill—the property of J. Turnbull Esq General R. E. Lee's head-quarters near Petersburg, Va." This sketch is the only known likeness of Lee's last headquarters before the retreat to Appomattox. Before the discovery of the Conolly diary, the only visual representation of the building was a drawing of the ashes that remained after the farmhouse burned in the evacuation of Petersburg. *Castletown Foundation*

gold band his immediate staff Col. Taylor, Col Venables, Col Pegram[53] Artillery He standing aloof evidently a conference before action. Lee on a broken

officer was still in North Carolina. Conolly probably was referring to William Nelson Pendleton (1809–1883), brigadier general, C.S.A.

[53]William Ransom Johnson Pegram (1841–1865), artillery colonel, killed at Five Forks two days later (William W. Hassler, " 'Willie' Pegram: General Lee's Brilliant Young Virginia Artillerist," *Va. Cavalcade*, XXIII [Autumn 1973], 12–19). Footnote: "Col. Pegram is brother to Genl Pegram that married the beautiful Miss Carey of Baltimore & was killed a week after!!!"

Major Giles Buckner Cooke (1838–1937), of Lee's staff, escorted
Conolly about the Petersburg battlefield and, finding him a fascinat-
ing conversationalist, described the visitor as "an Englishman who
came over to this country to see what could be seen." *Virginia Historical Society*

fence the others round him while some officer is drawing a plan of the
ground with a stick in the mud, all looking on while he describes the position of the enemy Lee takes the stick & assigns to each Genl his position on
the mud map—Then a pause & seeing me he calls me to his side an hour
elapses while they discuss pro & con then 2 or 3 genls start up & proceed to
the head of their respective Divisions & move slowly on. Picket firing in the
woods in advance very heavy Genl Lee gives me a bit of bread & some Sar-
dines & we set down on our hunkers to discuss it with Taylor Venables &
Ransom—

This is nearly the same position as the battle fought by Grant & Meade[54] last September & there is a tree on the enemy's side near Gravelly run[55] where the Yankee Genls stood during that fight called Grants Tree The enemy hold Gravelly run & parallel to our Lines up to White Oak road. Genl Lee gets on his horse & with his Genl of Artillery Anderson & his personal staff rides quietly down the line to Burgess Mill placing guns on partic. points & strengthening others as he goes couriers come dashing up & deliver verbal messages or hand Taylor a slip of paper to wh he replies on his horse paper & pen in his holster. The picket firing continues merrily & the wounded being brought in on litters shows that the enemy is there This goes on more hotly near Burgess' Mill at the E. End of the Position where some heavy guns also play on the enemy from this we can see the Yankees about 1200 yds under Grants Tree & he can see us as that bullet says wh passes close by & hits a tree—& now the firing relaxes & the reports are brought in Enemy driven out his Lines in the upper part of the skirmish but holds to his Pickets at Hatchers run.[56] Home with Genl Lee—The rain had contd without interruption all day & one time when the firing was most hot He said to me is it not dreadful that these honest fellows should have to go through all this for their Independence—!! Truly he is a noble-hearted man—He canters along on his fine grey horse which he has ridden for 16 hours & yet he goes as fresh as a kitten! Dinner with Genl & his old Madeira again, I am wringing wet but eat a good dinner & get on old Grant again after dinner to make my way to Pryor's pitch dark all very well till I get to the stream[57] wh was so small in the morning I find it flowing like the Appomattox 20 yds wide so hesitating a moment on the bank I resolve to go it & sticking both spurs in charge into the flood. down goes old Grant but struggling well with the

[54]George Gordon Meade (1815–1872), commander of the Army of the Potomac (*Blue*, pp. 315–17).

[55]The engagement at Burgess's Mill or Boydton Plank Road, 27 October 1864 (*Almanac*, pp. 589).

[56]Wilcox recalled that Conolly "witnessed the collision between Col. Ashford, commanding two North Carolina regiments, and a small force of the enemy. This pleased him so much that he offered his services to me for the coming campaign, and said if I would permit him he would remain with me until its close. I accepted his tender of service, and told him I would make him one of my volunteer aids. He thanked me, and asked if I would let him go under fire. I replied that it would hardly be possible for him to escape being under fire. He said he would return to Richmond, get his baggage and report to me early Monday morning. He left me Saturday evening. Our lines were broken next morning, and the army retired towards Appomattox" (*SHSP*, IV, 22n). According to Conolly, he left on Friday, not Saturday. Of his offer of service, he made no mention.

[57]Conolly would have had to cross Rohoic Creek, which flows into the Appomattox River, to travel the mile between Lee's headquarters and the Pryors's house.

Part of the Confederate defenses at Petersburg, photographed one day after they were abandoned by Lee's army and four days after Conolly's last visit to the lines. *Library of Congress*

waves he snuffles & swims & clambers & pushes thro' the brush till we get up safe out not much wetter than before so on to Pryors, find Mrs Pryor as usual at her work. Pryor & Wilcox come in & I excuse myself & go to bed & get John the nigger to dry my clothes & call me at 4 next morning.

Friday, 31 March

When up I find nothing can be done about getting on my boots so get a pair of mockassins from Wilcox & start on old Grant with my boots & spurs

slung before me wet morg & pitch dark. Charles on a mule with me thro'
Petersburg where it begins to get light & thence on to train at Dunlop! Find
[Bench?] in train sleep quietly all the way to Richmond. Breakfast & wash &
dress clean & then go to look after our party to Drury's Bluff with Nannie
Thomas & Mrs. Guest[58] & find the Freshet is great in River & we cannot go so
order dinner in Mrs Thomas room Mrs Guest sings Dinner waited on by my
boy Henry!—Cocktails in my room with McCann Lawley arrives in Stringers
room Evening with smoke & mint juleps, Point Dexter, Lawly, D'Orsay Cullen,[59] Watson[60] Stringer, self adjourn to my room & repeat. &c &c—

SATURDAY, 1 APRIL

Get some more money![61] Pay Bill at Hotel & other small things Old Tom
Griffin for yesterdays feast. Send for my horse Vixen & out to see Goree &
Longstreet Confab. with Longstreet & go over the whole map with him. One
of his A.D.C. bring in a Spencer rifle & asks his opinion on it. Fires 7 times &
loads in the stock.! He does not like it Thinks it would make men unsteady
thinks one shot sufficient, men are too much inclined to throw away their
fire—His honest bluff countenance & thorough soldierlike appearance. His
stories of Buffalo hunting &c. [He?] is called the Bull Dog of the army & a finer
specimen of a sterling hard-fighter you cannot see one of his arms is stiff from a
shot thro' the muscles, but he says it is getting better & does not trouble
him—Maurice Kavanagh is high in his confidence Mr Maurice among the niggers—! 2 cocktails with Genl Longstreet & 2 cigars—I dine with Goree & the
staff little Alexander & 2 others capital bean soup & the usual bacon & corn
bread. Back full tilt at 4 for Nannie Thomas & find her & the green habit all
right saddle the grey horse & start out the same way at a swing canter we are

[58]Malvina Black Gist wrote in her diary for 30 March, "Indeed, something very serious is
astir in military circles. After arranging everything, the M.P. has had to give up the projected
outing on the James? It is not safe—a fight is brewing." The next day she wrote, "Mr. Connelly
gave us a collation in the hotel in lieu of the abandoned picnic. Very swell, despite the blockade.
Must have cost him a pretty sum" (in Jones, ed., *Heroines of Dixie*, p. 383).

[59]John Syng Dorsey Cullen (1832–1893), a Richmond surgeon, held several prominent
medical positions during the war, including acting medical director of the Army of Northern
Virginia (Blanton, *Medicine*, p. 121).

[60]At least since 1863, L. G. Watson had been an agent for London companies engaged in
blockade running. He was known to Heyliger, the Confederate agent at Nassau whom Conolly
met there (*OR*, ser. iv, II, 633–35, 852). Conolly met Watson again in New York City. See entry
for 22 April. Signature at back of diary: "L G Watson B R Reform Club London."

[61]As on 22 March, he exchanged a bill for £50 with Branch, Morton & Co. but never with-
drew all of the funds in his account. When the firm liquidated in July 1865 it owed him
$12,399.99—in Confederate currency (Ledger Book 1865, Branch & Co., Richmond, Va.,
Records, VHS).

On the morning of 3 April, Conolly witnessed the destruction begin in Richmond: "Then the awful shock the magazine exploded There is the death knell of Richmond & then another & then another ... and now the plundering begins." In this print the last Confederate troops pass over Mayo's Bridge as the flames engulf the business district of the city. *Library of Congress*

This photograph, taken from the Spotswood, captures the view he could have seen from one of his hotel's windows, had Conolly remained in Richmond a few more days. By the time the ashes of these buildings around Capitol Square had cooled, however, the M.P. had fled northward to the Potomac. *Virginia Historical Society*

back at Longstreets at 5.15 and after a merry chat go on towards Genl
Gearys mistake Fields[62] quarters for Gearys & make our way back just as it
gets dark—Goodbye Nannie we go to Church tomorrow dont we oh yes
with pleasure up to drink [*illegible*] of Champagne & wait for McCann
who takes me up to Branches at Old Patteson sends his regards to his son
at Liverpool On to Mrs. Enders[63] find them all dancing 2 very pretty girls
& Miss Johnston a rare beauty & others making a merry party Messrs Taylor brothers to Col Taylor[64] at Genl Lees & others dance all round curious
quadrilles unlike anything I ever saw a sort of country dance.! Miss Mary
Enders plays beautifully & can play anything from ear without knowing
her notes—Stay with them dancing &c till 12. little did we know what a
day would bring forth.[65]

Sunday, 2 April[66]

Go to Church with Miss T. one of the most beautiful mornings I ever saw
in my life & sit between her & little Miss Enders, the others Enders just
before us Miss Sallie & Miss Mary. But what is the matter the sexton having
stealthily whispered to Jeff. Davis he rises & leaves the Ch then the same
operation to one & a second member of the Govt both follow suit, people
begin to whisper, when as if curiosity long suppressed had ignited they
rose (the whole congregation) in tens & 20 & left the Church, outside the
secret was soon abroad a telegram of Disaster at Hatcher's run line broken
by masses of the Enemy in 3 places Richmond must be evacuated signed R.

[62]Probably Charles William Field (1828–1892), major general, C.S.A. (*Gray*, pp. 87–88).

[63]"The home of Mrs John Enders was perhaps the pivotal point of gay and happy times for the
younger set. . . . Mrs. Enders was the friend of every boy who wore the gray" (De Leon, *Belles*, p.
148).

[64]Walter Herron Taylor, with whom Conolly had dined at Lee's headquarters on 16
March.

[65]Conolly wrote this passage at least several days later. The following entry, for Sunday, 2
April, was written on pages that were inserted and not part of the original diary. Conolly left
in the bound ledger space only for the title of the passage he intended to insert later on the
events of 2 April, "Crisis of Richmonds Fate."

[66]On 2 April Capt. Frank Potts, of Longstreet's staff, met Conolly just after learning of Lee's
plan to evacuate Petersburg: "It is eleven o'clock, the church bells are ringing, and thousands
are on their way to worship. I didn't go. I mounted, and as I was riding off Mr. Connolly, M.P. for
Donegal, then in Richmond, asked me to come and dine with him that evening, but, much to my
regret I had to beg off" (Frank Potts, *The Death of the Confederacy. . .* , ed. by Douglas Southall
Freeman [Richmond, 1928], p. 7).

E. Lee Then painful rumours follow thick on one another A P. Hill[67] killed, Fitzhugh Lee, great carnage, Petersburg in the hands of the Yanks &c &c, and as the day goes on the confirmation of all! The Govt officials all leave for Danville by train. Streets filled with departures, a regular stampede has begun. Go up to see Mrs Enders her nice pretty daughters are in a state of distraction I offer my services as they have no man with them I should be [indeed?] very much obliged to you Mr Conolly if you would stay with us thro' the night Oh we dread those terrible Enemies Then Stringer & Lawley & Watson with whom I dined at Tom Griffins arrange a hurried Departure & we take a parting cup to our next merry meeting Brave old Richmond to be given up! Oh 'sad fate after her faithful, courageous, watchful defence of 4 years & 100 battles, after drawing the life blood of chivalry & the hopes of families in her defence & bringing down her most lofty citizens to poverty well nigh threadbare in endurance you must at last bow to the hated nay accursed foe! Alas for your once proud device sic semper tyrannis![68] you now yourself fairest city of fair Virginia to be trodden under the boot of the ruthless & implacable Enemy! Oh it is hard, hard, hard for your men whose brave comrades have died for honor to see their noble city given up, still more hard for those high-souled Ladies who never hitherto dispaired who witnessed gigantic hosts hurled back from their gates & lived in the midst of the thunders of cannon for 4 years—hearing them grow weaker & weaker till each campaign closed with victory & safety & had thro such scenes erected for themselves a fancied invincibility for the City they loved & praised. to see or hear that it is to be given up They cannot believe it—Heaven will interfere. it never can be! But lo the hour approaches & as the last soldiers come up to take a long adieu perhaps for ever The long pent up tide of Emotions bursts forth & the poor girls fling themselves on down on their sofas & chairs & weep & sob 'till their hearts seem breaking. Oh it is a hard hard fate and at last at 4 o'clock a.m. They consent to go to bed utterly wearied out while I stay & watch Then the awful shock the magazine exploded There is the death knell of Richmond & then another & another and sure it was so—I went out & what a sight at that hour the streets filled with all the ragamuffins cheifly niggers running & hurrying about & then another crash another explosion & all the windows of the Spottswood are rent asunder as also of all the stores in Main Street & now the plundering begins men & women grabbing more than they can carry & bustling on under their burthens now the mills are on fire & the

[67]Ambrose Powell Hill (1825–1865), lieutenant general, C.S.A., killed in the fall of Petersburg (see James I. Robertson, Jr., *General A. P. Hill: The Story of a Confederate Warrior* [New York, 1987]). The reports of Fitzhugh Lee's death were in error.

[68]"Thus always to tyrants," the motto of the Commonwealth of Virginia.

crowd rush to get the flour & begins rolling out barrels thro' the street & carrying bags & sacks of flour the white meal & the black ashes making the nigger face most damnably ludicrous, hurry & bustle & noise everywhere I push & elbow my way down to say goodbye to Miss Thomas find her in tears her beautiful face quite swelled with weeping! A sad adieu, & as I go back to the Hotel the cry the Yankees![69]

[69]Footnote: "We were to have had a dinner of 12, Breckinridge, Benjamin, Myers, Col. Johnston, Lawley, T. C. Stringer Watson Point Dexter, and D'Orsay Cullen." Conolly's addition was faulty. Benjamin was probably Judah P. Benjamin (1811–1884), Confederate secretary of state (*DAB*, II, 181–86). In faint pencil near this footnote Conolly made some notes about his experiences in the first days after leaving Richmond, suggesting that he did not compose the section on the fall of the city until several days after the fact.

CHAPTER FOUR

"THE FLIGHT INTO EGYPT"

MONDAY, 3 APRIL[1]

My wafaring companions are all officers making for Lynchburg among whom I am at once a friend thro Col Brown of the Ordnance at Richmond whom I had met at Mrs Masons gives me a feed for my horse at the first halt 15 miles from R. & some rolls as I had no breakfast likewise a pouch of Tobacco—we part there I going to the right for Fredericksburg Rd & Bowling Green[2] & travel on alone thro' interminable forest all day 'till my horse can go no farther find out at a forge that there is a man of the name of Garnett near Morris ferry on the North Anna[3] & make for his house the greater part of the route I find traces of Sheridans raiding party dead horses in a state of putrefaction at every turn I passed 20. Mrs De Garnetts house was already full of Children of Israel like myself who are compelled to flee into Egypt Col Tayloe[4] among others struck up a friendship with me & offered to buy my

[1]On the sheet of paper inserted into the diary containing Conolly's account of the fall of Richmond are penciled some notes about the first days of his flight northward: "Mrs D is a widow Lady with 4 daughters. K. & Q. County. Whipped & Infant child killed because named Jeff. Davis dashed its brains out in presence of its mother. Mrs. King Spotsylvania (sister lives in Richmond)—Mrs Boulwere widow scared her to death telling her that they had hung her son & brandished a sword over her head she died on the spot. Mrs Burruss. Caroline. Boulwere—another killed in same manner. Bowling Green Caroline Va. Catharine Burruss Caroline Va.

[2]Bowling Green, Caroline County seat, about 35 miles north of Richmond and 10 miles southwest of Port Royal.

[3]On a Confederate engineer's map is a notation on the North Anna River for "Morris's Ford" (Gilmer map, Caroline County, 1863, VHS).

[4]John Tayloe V (1818–1873), of Windsor and Chatterton, King George Co., was a captain, not a colonel, in the 9th Virginia Cavalry. He was captured in 1862, released, resigned for ill health, captured again, and released only on 2 February 1865. In support of his resignation, the governor had written that Tayloe had lost his slaves, his crops, and his wealth and that his house had been shelled from the Potomac (W. Randolph Tayloe, *The Tayloes of Virginia and Allied*

85

horse & buggy on my arrival at Port Royal[5] at Supper we were joined by a pretty lady[6] who was journeying with her negro servants & children in a waggon & an ambulance drawn by mules They had been 2 days getting here having camped out the first night under the protection of Col. Tayloe whom they picked up on the way She was going to Culpepper—her husband was with the army under Genl Lee—

TUESDAY, 4 APRIL

Started after Bk giving Mrs De Garnett one of my gold shirt studs for her hospitality & buying some strong cake Tobacco from her negro cook for 50 doll. Confed money—Col. Tayloe agrees to go with me & gives me 100 doll. in gold or greenbacks to that amt. for horse & Buggy at Port Royal[7]

We soon found that my poor horse had got nothing the night before & & being quite dead tired when I arrived last night & quite empty ever since soon began to show signs of Resignation we had gone only 5 miles & crossed by Morris ferry when a long hill stopped him & we began to cast about for help & providentially lighted upon a comfortable farmer one Freeman who fed my poor horse for me Mrs Freeman related sad stories of the Yankee depradations in passing, having stripped her poor house, broken her little crockery & taken all her poultry, hogs, & cattle as well as their only horse— She gave a similar account of her neighbors, those who had relatives in the Confed. army faring worst. Mr Hunter[8] relative of the Peace commssr & Senator lost everything as they sent before them 2 men dressed in Confed. Uniforms who advised him to secrete his horses & he said he had already done so & told where they were They were shortly followed by an invasion of many Yanks who were directed by these Spies & took the horses & everything on his extensive plantation breaking agric. implements and all they cd not carry away—Pushed on to Reda Mill on the Appotomye[9] & found that fine mill wrecked & the people lamenting bitterly over the fall of Richmond—As we passed several Ladies ran out from their houses all in grief inconsolable for this dreadful calamity & all asking tidings from the army

Families [Berryville, Va., 1965], pp. 27–28; Robert Krick, *9th. Virginia Cavalry*, The Virginia Regimental Histories Series [Lynchburg, Va., 1982], p. 101).

[5]Port Royal, in Caroline County on the south bank of the Rappahannock River, about 45 miles north of Richmond.

[6]Footnote: "Mrs. Wood."

[7]See entry for 21 April.

[8]Possibly James Hunter, first cousin of Confederate Peace Commissioner R. M. T. Hunter.

[9]Conolly garbled two names here. He meant Ready's Mill on the Mattaponi River (Gilmer map, Caroline County, 1863, VHS).

from corps in wh their husbands & sons were serving—Pushed on from Reda mills for Bowling Green but our poor horse gave up. met some artillery soldiers who had pulled up their trowsers to ford a creek on the road & 3 out of 4 showed marks of severe wounds in their legs they were fine young fellows lately out of hospital who had been cut off from their regt by the burning of Mayo bridge[10] at Richmond & had pushed on with the intention of joining the force at Lynchburg—We enquired from a lady in a buggy where we could go for our nightly lodging & found an excellent hostess in Mrs Burruss[11] whose cheer was first rate tho' her acct of Yankee depradations & cruelties was surpassing all we had heard before. She has a son in the army & her whole soul in the cause many war-stained & weary soldiers dropped in during the night & all were well received & fed—She gave us some excellent home made wine & apple brandy & her table was covered with rustic profusion notwithstanding the losses of 20 head of cattle 20 hogs & quantities of household stuff bacon fowl &c. &c Old Burruss was a stiff old codger of slow manner but kind & well disposed—I gave her my name & one of my ivory brushes with the crest & initial wh she seemed to prize—

WEDNESDAY, 5 APRIL

Off at 8 next morning after a comfortable rest Tayloe & I occupying same bed. get along famously 15 miles, to Bowling Green & much entertained by the Companionship of a wonderful smart boy of 15 Maurice Roe whose father was a Commissary formerly a butcher from Fredericksburg This young lad had charge of droves of cattle & negroes for his father & was in the habit of taking long journeys thro' the country all parts of wh he seemed to know His horse a powerful brown had lately been bought for his brother who was with the famous Mozeby[12] & I am going to him too as soon as father lets me Brothers bay mare is coming home & he is to have Jock viz this brown horse—But he could not go our pace so wished us Luck & striking into a hard gallop was out of sight in a jiffy

Made Bowling Green found more traces of the Yankee army burnt houses & fed our horse—proceeded for Port Royal.

[10]Mayo's Bridge across the James River, burned by the last Confederate troops to evacuate Richmond.

[11]"G. Burrow's" house was located just north of Ready's Mill (Gilmer map, Caroline County, 1863, VHS).

[12]John Singleton Mosby (1833–1916), leader of the 43d Battalion Partisan Rangers (*DAB*, XIII, 272–73).

Stopped again from the exhausted state of our horse at the Trap 1/2 way to Port Royal where we find Mrs Carter[13] & her 4 pretty daughters the house was full of Virginia Cavalry going to join their Regts & the girls & mother serving them all round with all they had—Got some dinner bacon & greens & pickled peaches & corn bread & milk—Matty[14] & I had a pleasant chat & I gave her the other gold stud wh pleased her much.

Push on again for Port Royal and arrive at Mr Gibbs at 9 as we had mistaken our route about a mile from the village & gone 3 miles wrong with our unhappy jaded horse—We had great difficulty & severe beating to get him to the wished for Hostelrie, we went immediately to bed Col. Tayloe & I occupying same bed in a small room with side door opening to back yard Slept well & rose refreshed. Excellent Bk of Shad, coffee, & corn bread. much entertained by Mrs Gibbs to whom I promised a calico dress—

THURSDAY, 6 APRIL

Across the Rappahannock & after a short visit to Mr Farmer make a successful journey 16 miles to this delightful place[15] over the Potomac commanding extensive views up & down that Lordly River up to Acquia Creek & Potomac creek,[16] & all the splendid woodland scenery around with the broad bosom of the Noble river at the bottom of a long sloping bank of a furlong in distant the whole view shut in by the line of the blue ridge Mts[17] on the left & the forests of Maryland in front. Col. & Mrs Tayloe[18] & their dear little children[19] Lucy Kate & Minnie with my friend Forest of the flaxen locks & clear bright eyes make me feel quite at home & enjoy much the perfect peace of this beautiful situation & all its picturesque accessories after the troubles & agonies, & toil & warfare out of which we have emerged. Truly it seems like enchantment to find oneself so quickly removed to this beautiful serene atmosphere of home & tranquillity.

[13]Martha Carter and daughters Mary (Molly), Martha (Mattie), Sarah, and Agnes, operated this well-known tavern and place of entertainment, about half way between Bowling Green and Port Royal (James O. Hall, "The Trappe," *Surratt Courier* [June 1987]).

[14]Martha (Mattie) Carter was about 27 years old.

[15]Tayloe's estate, Chatterton, in King George Co., Virginia.

[16]Acquia Creek and Potomac Creek empty into the Potomac on the Virginia side a few miles upstream from Chatterton.

[17]It is questionable whether Conolly could have seen the Blue Ridge Mountains, about 60 miles west of Chatterton.

[18]Mary Willis Lewis (1824–1885) married John Tayloe in 1855 (Merrow Egerton Sorley, comp., *Lewis of Warner Hall* . . . [Baltimore, 1979], p. 183).

[19]Forrest Plater (1860–1930), Lucy Daingerfield (b.1858), Catherine Attaway (b.1861), and Maria Bohrer (d.1886).

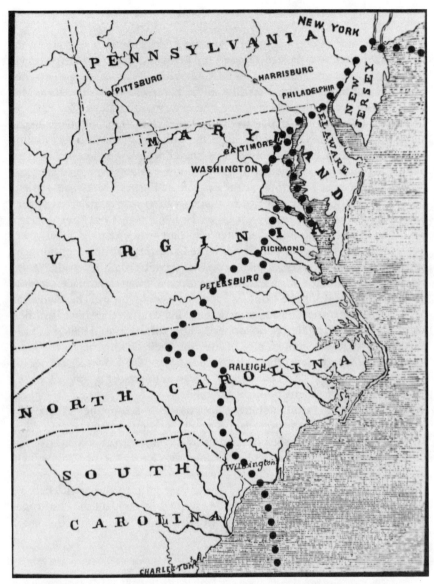

Thomas Conolly's American itinerary, shown by the line of dots plotted on an adaptation of an 1861 map from *Harper's Weekly*.

FRIDAY, 7 APRIL

Most refreshing sleep, got up to Enjoy more than ever the rising sun on the glorious Potomac.—Give Col Tayloe[20] my Russian chain of gold & platina in token of his valued Friendship—And General R. E. Lee & his noble army! They have suffered, we hear terribly in the battle of Sunday The little Miss Lucas[21] from Petersburg whom I met when I went up to see Lawley & Co off to Fredericksburg on Monday morning[22] said that the Cannonade began along the entire line on Saturday night the same as on the last occasion on Wed the 29th Inst. (q.v) & was kept up the entire night when half an hour before day musketry opened & 3 heavy columns of attack charged the lines on 3 diff. places at [*illegible*] at the Dam & at Burgess' Mill, The 1st succeeded & on they came right thro' Wilcox's head quarters sacked Pryor's house, poor Mrs Pryor barely escaping & right on to Genl Lees quarters which were also sacked his daughter also narrowly escaping—This awful fight (it seems continued all Sunday till Longstreet about 3 coming up effected a change in favor of the Confeds & terrific slaughter ensued *These are the rumours* since wh we heard that more fighting took place on Monday with a success for the Confeds! And now for the future The Campaign has altered its features considerably & the Confeds altho they have lost their far-famed city & Capital have no longer 36 miles of works to defend but have the long wished for opportunity of meeting their deadly foe *in the Field* "Awa to the woods & to the hills to the Rocks/ "Ere I own a usurper I'd crouch with the Fox/ "And tremble fa' Whigs in the midst o' your glee/ "Ye ha nae' seen the last o' my bonnets and me.!

No the stars of the Confederacy temporarily Eclipsed by the last splendid sacrifice! must rise in the ascendant & yet make the world grow pale—The finest army that ever was seen has had its own country to fight in against terrible odds but that is no new thing for them & Victory Victory Victory will soon crown its constancy & Virtue!—

Breakfast with Col. & Mrs Tayloe & the dear little children who call me "John Bull" especially little Forest & then write & scratch 'till the rain comes on which lasts till evening—Lucky to get thro our journey with our jaded

---

[20]Appendix: "Tayloe's coat of arms Chatterton. Potomac."

[21]See entry for 8 April for Henry Lucas. Was Miss Lucas a relation?

[22]Lawley wrote that as he left Richmond for Fredericksburg the fires in the business district were beginning: "As the train moved off from the Fredericksburg depot about 6 o'clock I parted with Mr. Connolly, the member for Donegal, who had passed a month in Richmond, and was upon this eventful morning still undecided whether to follow General Lee's army or to strike northwards like myself." Conolly did not mention his indecision (Hugh Brogan, ed., *The Times Reports the American Civil War: Extracts from the Times, 1860–1865* [London, 1975], p. 168).

horse before this rain—Nice job that would have been, I can imagine his meager frame & lopping ears & drooping head in the middle on one of the red mud wallows, wheels fixed up to the axels, & the unhappy travellers chewing their misfortunes with the rain streaming down their back bone! Jolly very Jolly a very pretty how dye do! Thank you—Just as well as it is—Good night Two more young Ladies come this Evening Miss Lewis, & Miss Ashton[23]

SATURDAY, 8 APRIL

After Bk at Chatterton got directions for Conrads[24] camp & go for clearer instructions up to the Quarters to old Uncle Leon find him lying very ill & 'dont know nuffin' bout Conrads But May Ann a yellow negress directs little Cornelius a one-eyed imp to show me the way to Mrs Jeters[25] "whar youll hear on him Sartain"—3 miles over the wooded hills till we came up the river Bank then several ploughed fields till the next cottage comes in view with its offices avenue of trees orchards & comely porch Peach trees in full blossom & ladies standing in the shade of the Porch Mrs Jeter & her daughters to whom I explain my business She calls Mr Daly[26] an Irishman who at once opens Tayloe's letter to Conrad & then after Daly perusing it hands it back to me 'He will be here directly' There he is coming down the hill on horseback & arrives a very handsome man of olive complexion, light wiry figure, black frockcoat, clasped belt pistols, boots & spurs & black slouch hat with feather Capt Conrad tying up his horse to the rack is met by Daly who tells me to wait till he sees the Capt He advances straight to me & greets me with such manner & frankness & 'I shall be happy to take you across tonight I then give him my letter 'All right' [*illegible*] he after 1/2 hours chat the war agrees to meet me at Tayloes landing at 9 tonight "All right" and bidding an adieu to the Ladies I hasten back with Cornelius to pack up—Take leave of

[23]Footnote: "Mrs. Tayloe's sister"; Attaway Miller Lewis (1829–1915) (Sorley, comp., *Lewis of Warner Hall*, p. 186). Footnote: "see names in List Appx"; signatures at back of diary: "Attie Lewis" and "Ella Ashton."

[24]Thomas Nelson Conrad was a Confederate chaplain and spy who operated with great success throughout the war from his base along the Potomac. A week after ferrying Conolly across the Potomac he was arrested making the same trip on suspicion of being John Wilkes Booth, still at large after having shot Lincoln (John Bakeless, *Spies of the Confederacy* [Philadelphia and New York, 1970], pp. 66–74).

[25]Probably Agnes Jeter, whose family of five daughters and one son was the only one of that surname in King George County in the 1860 census. Conrad mentioned in his memoir that one of his associates was a Lieutenant Jeter.

[26]Daly was Conrad's oarsman for his expeditions along the Potomac (M. Clifford Harrison, "A Fighting Confederate Chaplain Spy," *Va. Cavalcade*, XII, no. 4 [1963], 21).

Col. & Mrs Tayloe & their dear children & Forest Miss Lewis, & Mrs Sythe (sis of Geo Fitzhugh) & then proceed to my station—There at 1/4 9—10—11—Lie down on Shingle & count stars & listen to the heavy laboring of the giant Steamers & watch the flickering signal lights as they correspond along the Maryland shore, at last getting very cold in the moon-light take a walk on the top of the bank overlooking the bay & seeing no approach decide on hiding my luggage & repair along the shore to Mrs Jeters 4 miles If by chance I can make her out by the vague light with its heavy shadows—so trudge away thro the heavy sand thinking either to see the boat or make out the people or at all events to keep warm till morning—along by the sad plashing waves of the Potomac, fine moonlight banks & trees looming large in the shadows & old stumps & peices of wreck taking all manner of fantastic shapes look at my watch after walking an hour & coming up to some Tenement or "Cottage by the Sea" No this wont do I'm not far enough trudge on as it were the 4 miles Then the next dont look like it Farm ho. too large other buildings I dont recognize as I had not seen it from the water after a little more travel & deliberation continue my course but find the bank get low & swampy & the fields come down to the beach unlike the sloping orchard & avenue of trees I saw this morng. Also the headland appears nearer than it ought so Consulting my watch I decide on trying the land attack of the last Position & strike into the country for this purpose so half an hour & I make out the avenue barn & orchard & lastly the low cottage & porch wh stands like a T across & in front of the larger house All right there is the seat where the Ladies were now to get in! So here goes rap at the door I soon hear a movement inside Mrs Jeter is sitting up with her sick daughter & soon opens a lower window & recognizes me—"Capt Conrad started but was obliged to put back" I will call him Daly comes down & opens the door & lets me in 'can I stay' Oh yes There's room for you & he shows me thro' the Cottage up stairs in the large back building to a spacious upper appartment occupied by 4 men & Capt Conrad. All asleep, "you can go into the Capts bed & he vaults into his comrades lair—I wake Conrad & ask his permission to introduce my cold body into his warm nest 'All right' I was soon asleep & very good bed it was next day Sunday[27] All up at 6 & Conrad who is a preacher as well as a daring adverturer reads a Chapter & then prays extempory (after Presbytr manner) very good language & fervid address—Bk dispensed by good Mrs Jeter & her daughter thorough Confeds. had suffered much from the Yankees but staunch—excellent homemade bread, butter, eggs, fish shad! nigger servants as usual in Virginia!—Several people call during the day & Conrad after Bk puts on his belt, pistols & Chapeau Plumé & rides off to minister at a Ch.

[27]Conolly should have marked the entry for Sunday, 9 April, beginning after this point.

some 6 miles off, preparatory to this Evg work Among the guests was pretty Miss Anna [*illegible*] who comes on horseback in a pretty habit trimmed with red & her swain a Confed soldier on furlough (I like the way these Confed. women trust themselves implicitly to the high feeling of their male companions) I wish it was so in Europe, it would be much better—Another Henry Lucas[28] brings news from Fredericksburg of good import *tho 'vague'* Pleasant dinner with all these jolly folk 12 in all—Lucas is quite a wag & very pleasant was with J. E B Stuart & wounded in knee & head, larks with the girls & says it is the only thing he's fit for & he has earned his right to kiss— Then arrives another cavalry furlough also suffering from a wounded leg & riding his well-caparisoned spirited [mount?] with his crutch in the rest like a lance long Texan spurs red pointed beard, jack boots & Chapeau plumé something Quixotic in his get up with Yankee light-blue Gt Coat The Yankees have clothed the Entire Country with these Excellent light blue great coats, me included!—All these start off different directions after Tea[29] & message comes from Capt Conrad to meet him at night at 10 at Boyds hole[30] Bid Mrs Jeter[31] & her kind daughters good bye thank them for their hospitality—

Drop down quietly with muffled oars to my ambush where I had secreted my goods & getting them noiselessly aboard proceed to the Rendezvous, look at watch 10 we pull hard to make time In half an hour we are at Boyds Hole 10.30 where we descry one fig. on the beach by a log house at a signal given[32] we row in & Conrad [accosts us?] armed to the teeth[33]

[28]Footnote: "Lucas gives me address of his mother in Baltimore."

[29]Unknown to Conolly and the others, the steamer carrying President Lincoln back to Washington—he had visited Richmond immediately after its fall—passed by during the day (Earl Schenck Miers, ed. in chief, *Lincoln Day by Day: A Chronology, 1809–1865*, Vol. III, C. Percy Powell, ed., *1861–1865* [Washington, D.C., 1960], p. 327).

[30]Conrad established his headquarters for ventures onto the Potomac at Boyd's Hole, some miles downstream from Chatterton (Thomas Nelson Conrad, *The Rebel Scout*... [Washington, D.C., 1904], pp. 92–95).

[31]Footnote: "Mrs Jeter's apprehensions for the night Expedition if they should do any thing lest it should be visited on her by the Yanks while her daughters illness cont. If she was well I wouldn'd care you could fire away!!—"

[32]Footnote: "claps his hands 3 times!"

[33]Conrad wrote his memoirs nearly 40 years after the war. If the tricks played by time and memory are taken into account, perhaps the following story was his account of meeting Conolly: "In January, 1865, I received instructions from Richmond stating that an Englishman of eminence would be in Fredericksburg on a certain day, and that I must meet him, take him to my quarters, and on the first opportunity send him over the river to Maryland. I met him, brought him to Eagle Nest, and at night took him over to the Maryland shore. I heard afterward that he was an English lord, returning from an interview with the Confederate government, and

Sunday, 9 April[34]

Taking Daly aside for a little quiet converse then at a given signal 8 men emerge from the copse & take their places noiselessly in the boat stowing their arms along the gunnels Daly turns the boat & taking the stroke soon sends her at a rattling pace for Maryland. 30 min & we are off the Maryland shore Conrad keeping a look out from the bows & passing a whisper to change the course, another whisper & all oars are shipped & we wait in darkness & silence the next order, only a vessel aground! Give way & creep up along the shore—Stop opp. to Mr Ratcliffes[35] house & Daly & I have to wade out some 50 yds with the luggage. He gives me the cue & then leaves as they have an expedition on hand Ratcliffes house protected by fierce dogs who come furiously till he comes to the rescue & soon admits me to bed at 12.30 I got a Yankee coat from Daly in exchange for 450 dollars Confed. money—![36]

Monday, 10 April

After a family Bk with Mr & Mrs Ratcliffe & the handsome children (Mrs R. one of the nicest & handsomest women I ever saw, Go out with Henry her eldest son having first mended the market basket & made a handle for it with rope Take six dozen eggs & some milk to go up the river & trade with the fishermen for shad—& look out for a chance smack for Washington fall in with Capt Spalding[37] of the Abeona who wants a hand to work his schooner to Baltimore engage with him & stripping off my Yankee coat & jacket fall to work to get 50 fathom of anchor chains & 2 heavy anchors into a lighter & ship them aboard the schooner 2 hours hard work accomplished this task & another hour with the tackle in getting them into their berth—Then pull down to Ratcliffes for my things & after an affectionate adieu to Mrs R & give her one of my gold studs we pull up along the shore & take a load of drift wood Then to dinner with Capt Spalding & his damned Yankee mate of the accursed name of Seward, a fit specimen for the name all jaw & swagger— The cabin of the Abeona is a dark hole with a black stove & the housekeeping

---

the bearer of important papers to English brokers and bankers" (Conrad, *The Rebel Scout*, p. 148).

[34]Marginal note added later: "This day Genl Lee surrd."

[35]Probably Thomas M. Ratcliffe, whose wife was Susan America Ratcliffe. They were the only family of that name with a son named Henry in Charles County, Maryland, in the 1860 census.

[36]Two weeks later John Wilkes Booth crossed the Potomac almost at the same point, although going in the opposite direction, in flight from Washington.

[37]Probably Charles Clement Spalding (1822–1879), of St. Mary's Co., Maryland. For much of the war he had been under observation by the U.S. Navy as a suspect in the clandestine trade between Maryland and Virginia (*ORN*, ser. 1, V, 60–61).

is done by a very pretty girl called Juli who is black with dirt & smoke—Coffee very good, hot bread, bacon Juli & Johnny Paul her brother serve the dainty meal & they go ashore for fish while I smoke my pipe in the penetration of this murky cabin While July & Johnny clean up & [*illegible*] the ship singing nigger songs together—This arrangement suits me exactly for I am entirely devoid of money, having given all my Confed. notes to Daly!!! Capt & Seward arrive at 10.30 with fish, greens, & eggs & then to bed rats, rats, rats everywhere!—& a nigger in the berth under me—

TUESDAY, 11 APRIL

Up at 6. a.m & get the ship under weigh heaving the anchor (hard work) & setting the sails leave Maryland Pt[38] at 6.30. very light breeze on the quarter passed Pt Matthias[39] at 12 & lay up for the light wind failing & a strong tide against us cast anchor at 4 off the white [chimnies?]—

The Potomac here is a splendid river some 6 miles broad nearly opposite port Tobacco[40]—beautifully wooded on both sides to the water with beautiful bays garnished with trim fishing stations—The traffic in the river is very great carried on principally by taught handsome schooners for wh Baltimore is famous & the flying pungeys[41] Huge steamers pass & repass continually from Washington & the Chesapeake principally engaged in Govt transport & loaded with Soldiers, Prisoners ammunition & stores hay &c for the army on the James[42]—all these work with the walking beam engine—screw transports with horses all for the war!!!—Passed one of the famous Monitors steaming some 7 knots & covered with men, her aspect being of the quaintest as being quite flat you can see nothing at a dist. but her huge Gun towers & her smoke stack & steering box but her capacity below the water line is suff. for 500 men—On nearer approach we found the craft to be fully 300 feet long by 50 or 60 beam—Engines &c below the water line to the depth of 20 feet or more—This sort of Monitor same as fought at Hampton roads is preferable to those of Semmes fleet the Virginia Fredericksburg &c

[38]Maryland Point, in Charles Co., Maryland, directly opposite Chatterton.

[39]Conolly meant Mathias Point in King George Co.

[40]Port Tobacco, in Charles Co., Maryland, directly opposite Mathias Point.

[41]Footnote: "Pungey a light draft fast sailing schooner of small size for market purposes very pretty craft—" Pungy, a specifically Chesapeake term, refers to a vessel especially favored by oystermen.

[42]The Union army that had invested Richmond and Petersburg was supplied by water, and Conolly would have seen the supply transports on the Potomac.

as presenting no object for enemys mark & being able by the revolving tower to fire all round with the heaviest artillery, While they can only fire from their ports & have their crew in a state of suffocation while the gunnery is going on for want of ventilation. The Confeds had batteries on Pt Matthias the first 2 years of the war & harrassed the Federal gun boats much while they stopped all other traffic as the ship channel is commanded by their guns—Dinner & supper as before with some capital fish & greens under the care of the Arab Juli—

WEDNESDAY, 12 APRIL

Up at 6 dead calm—Get the fish & help Juli Paul to cook, & make bread for Bk smoke my last Pipe Tobacco running short—Grease my boots with some bacon fat Johnny Paul produces a small fit of black Tobacco. wh will do till we get a chance of more! Very blue look out for Baltimore! All day lie still a light breeze springing up, get sail on & weigh anchor & away before it getting fresher till we go along merrilie keep her at it & pass Pine Pt[43] & the mouth of the great Potomac into Chesapeake Bay then the guard ship— cachez vous et je me suis joliment cache[44] then passed Point Look out with its Steamers, gunboats barracks & last but not least the Prison where 30,000 Confeds are rotting[45]—storm comes down the bay strike us just as we get down our sails & we turn & run into Patuxan bay[46] just at dark made 80 miles in 7 hours! Better—Lie up at anchor snug—

THURSDAY, 13 APRIL

Up at 6 Raining dead calm stay quiet all day & go ashore for Tobacco & oysters. then finally to bed—Confer with Black Dick who expects a breeze tomorrow—

---

[43]Probably Piney Point, St. Mary's Co., Maryland, which the schooner would have passed shortly before reaching Point Lookout.

[44]Conolly's garbled French seems to say something like "Hide yourself and I hid myself nicely," but his meaning is unclear. Perhaps he meant it as a taunt to the guard ship.

[45]The North's largest prison camp, at the extreme southeastern tip of the western shore of Maryland (*ECW*, p. 588). Captain T. N. Conrad had been a prisoner there early in the war but escaped.

[46]Probably the Patuxent River. If the storm hit after rounding Point Lookout, the Patuxent would have been the first place to look for shelter on the western Bay shore.

Sailing down the Potomac to the Chesapeake Bay on the schooner *Abeona*, Conolly passed by Point Lookout, Maryland, where the Federal government maintained the largest of its camps for Confederate prisoners. Thomas N. Conrad, the rebel spy who ferried the M.P. across the Potomac, was a prisoner there earlier in the war but escaped. *National Archives*

FRIDAY, 14 APRIL

Get up all hands at 3. a.m. a breeze weigh & set sail before Black Dick is up pass[47] Cove Point light at 6.15—10 miles James Point at 7.15—20—Sharps Island—8.15—30—Poplar Island Kent Island—10.35. 40—Annapolis Sandy Point—1.10—55 Fort [Knowle?] 3.10 65 Fort Carrol 7. Breeze falls & cast anchor in Patapsaxa River[48] 7 miles below Baltimore

[47]Conolly would have passed these point in his journey up the Bay.
[48]The Patapsco River connects the Baltimore harbor with the Chesapeake Bay.

CHAPTER FIVE

"LENA UNPARALLELED LENA!"

SATURDAY, 15 APRIL

Weigh anchor at 1. a.m. and run up to Baltimore before Bk passing Fort McHenry & all the shipping arrive 7. a.m. Goodbye Juli & Johnny Paul Good bye Capt Spalding & your Yank mate Hear the news astounding.! President Lincoln was assassinated last night in the Theatre at Washington[1] This has paralyzed everything & all egress from the city N is stopped—accordingly I have time to look about me & visit Mrs Lucas[2] in W Fayette St Mother of Lucas of Mrs Jeters She tells me of Old Ward's House father of Frank Ward of Wilcox's staff (vide XIII p. 18)[3] & then go to Washington with Mrs Sullivan an Irish beauty whom I found in the Train Excellent supper & bed at the Depot & having ascertained my bearings after supper get out by 8 next morning to see the Capitol. Pennsylvania Av.—The White Ho. Treasury Long bridge &c—[4]

---

[1]Footnote: "See Appx in L. No24 et [*illegible*]." President Lincoln was shot on the evening of 14 April.

[2]In 1860 a William R. Lucas, of R. H. Lucas & Bro., flour and feed dealers, lived at 270 W. Fayette St., as did a Francis M. Lucas (*Wood's Baltimore City Directory* . . . [Baltimore, 1860]).

[3]On Conolly's page 18 of the diary, he recorded meeting, on 15 March, Francis Xavier Ward, whose father, William Ward, was a wealthy Baltimore merchant.

[4]Marginal note: "Drink a glass with old Ward on the occasion of Lincolns death to these Lines—Fill fill your glass the bottle pass/Let wine & tears both flow/And gentle gladness allay the sadness/Of this Dark day of woe//When you & I shall come to die/No crowd will mourn our lot/ So take this measure of sparkling pleasure/Since we must be forgot—//If lightning stroke the tallest oak/Or yonder hills hath slain/But uncomplaining trees remaining/Still drink the rain—// Then let us sip with grateful lip/The wine Martinez grows/A marble story for Abr'hams glory/ And this frail glass for Ours.—"

SUNDAY, 16 APRIL

Dine at Restaurant & as the place was all in a ferment about the murder of Lincoln I decided to go to Baltimore & put up at old Ward's. Pleasant evening & tea with the Wards Miss Blanche very nice & To bed at 11—very comfortable

MONDAY, 17 APRIL

Walk all over Baltimore wh is a fine city & busy place with lots of Shipping. train at 1.20—arrive at Philadelphia at 5 train has excellent smoking & eating room, also I am told capital sleeping cars—LaPiere Ho[5] is excellent replete with every Luxury & kept by 2 Irishmen by the name of Ward[6] who are partic civil. Go to see Mrs Sterrett[7] & find out where Lena Peters[8] lives. Good supper & cosy bed, determined to see Lena in the morning—!

TUESDAY, 18 APRIL

Go out with Mrs Sterrett in a carriage she shows me the park & principal streets very nice quiet women totally unsophisticated!!!!
Philadelphia is the finest city I have seen in America & has more stability, houses well built wide streets fine public buildings &c The people too are quiet & well conducted & have none of the Rowdy tendencys. rife in Baltimore Both these cities are considerable in business & Wealth Philadelphia being remarkable for the Splendor & variety of its shops & the rich costumes of its very pretty women no such thing as poverty in either & an immense world always in the streets. Indeed since the astounding news!! Every body has been in a frenzy & the universal sentiment is that of a National bereavement both towns have there houses properly draped with banners & mourning & here great taste has been exhibited in its decoration all business is suspended till after the funeral Thursday next but the feeling is unmistakable & universal nothing else talked of—No Southern Sentiment here altho Balti-

---

[5]The La Pierre House, on Broad Street below Chesnut Street.

[6]Signature at back of diary: "Michael Ward La Pierre House Philada May 1st 1865." Ward was listed as the proprietor of the La Pierre House in *McElroy's Philadelphia City Directory for 1860* ... (Philadelphia, 1860), p. 1035.

[7]Conolly had met her in Nassau. She apparently went on to the North by more conventional means than her husband and Conolly. See entries for 23 February, and 21, 22 April.

[8]Evelyn Willing Peters (1845–1886), a society beauty whom Conolly had met before, apparently in Europe. Called "a handsome, showy girl" by another diarist, she married Craig Wharton Wadsworth in 1869. See Nicholas B. Wainwright, ed., *A Philadelphia Perspective: The Diary of Sidney George Fisher* ... (Philadelphia, 1967), p. 466; W. C. Spruance, comp., *The Spruance Family* ... (Wilmington, Del., 1933).

more is more than divided on the subject at 2 go to Mrs Peters[9] in Locust St[10] & find Minnie the second[11] & Mrs Peters but no Lena after sitting for an hour expecting her to come in every moment I find she is in New York, Mein Gott! Mein Gott! Mrs Peters asks me to dine tomorrow! Perhaps Lena will be home in 4 days or so I hope you can stay to see her—! By Jove I will after coming all this way I believe you my boy! go there again after dinner at 7.30 & to my unexpressible joy who should come in but Lena & her New York friend Miss Wadsworth[12]—She recognizes me at once[13] and is looking more lovely than ever! Lena unparalleled Lena!—She is tired with her journey but I shall see her tomorrow at Dinner home to bed 11.30—Very happy!!!!!!! Mrs Peters is a noble dame of F.F.V. extraction[14] & her family is quite remarkable—Write up Journal till 2 to bed—after a glass with Mr Ward of real old Whiskey!—

WEDNESDAY, 19 APRIL

Up & Bk at 9—Read Booths letter to the Phil. Enquirer[15] write & draw sketches for Log, till 4 Then out to see the Funeral preparations—The entire town draped with black & stars & stripes everybody decorated with mourning badges representing Lincoln with a black ribbon or colors—The streets quite full of people well dressed all imbued with the sentiment of a great National calamity—Fine sight—Dress for dinner & repair to Mrs Peters at

[9]Maria Louisa Miller had married Francis Peters (1817–1861) in 1839 and had three other children besides the two daughters whom Conolly saw while in Philadelphia. He apparently had also met a son, Samuel W. M. Peters, in England (See Spruance, comp., *Spruance Family*).

[10]Address at the back of diary: "1315 Locust St."

[11]Lena's sister, Maria Bedinger Peters (d.1894).

[12]Nancy Wharton Wadsworth, daughter of Gen. James S. Wadsworth and Mary Craig (Wharton) Wadsworth (Alden Hatch, *The Wadsworths of the Genesee* [New York, 1959], p. 73). Her brother, Craig Wharton Wadsworth, married Lena Peters four years after Conolly's visit.

[13]Conolly obviously had met her before, but his other diaries give no indication when or where.

[14]Lena's father was the grandson of Thomas Willing, mayor of Philadelphia and brother-in-law of William Byrd III of Virginia (See Spruance, comp., *Spruance Family*). It is not known if Mrs. Peters was also descended from any of the First Families of Virginia.

[15]Footnote: "Booths letter showing his sentiments & long cherished sentiments agst President no doubt exists as to his being the murderer!!!—See L. No33 et [*illegible*]." John Wilkes Booth had written a letter in 1864 that spelled out his animosity toward Lincoln. The letter had been placed with papers kept by Booth's brother-in-law, who turned it over to Federal officials after the assassination. The letter was first published in the *Philadelphia Enquirer.*

6—party of 8 Butler[16] Dr Wilcocse,[17] Mr Angier,[18] Mrs Peters Lena Minnie & Miss Wadsworth also a very handsome person sis. to Mrs Ritchie[19] of famous beauty! Sit next to Lena & find my Position very Charming—Good dinner & pleasant friends Miss McCall come in Evg—& plays, Angier sings & Evg passes off with great glee—Go with Dr Wilcocse to Phil. Club where I am enrolled as a guest![20] read the London Papers till 1— Then to bed.

Thursday, 20 April

Went to see Mrs Sullivan[21] & give her Genl Lees portrait—The other two of Stonewall Jackson & Lee I gave to Mrs Peters—Then to Mrs Sterrett & find her in a state of restless anxiety not having heard from Stereotype in answer to her letters. Away to see the Peters where I find Miss Alice Potter sweet little blonde with the most cocky blue bonnet Lena was out with Miss Wadsworth & I had a small chat with Minnie & then comes Angier hollering loudly for me we go off with little Willy to see the race course & Flora Temple the other horses are worth seeing but Flora is the most remarkable animal I ever saw exhibiting in extraordinary depth & symmetry all the qualifications & points of an old Irish cob mare with a cock tail fine head beautiful eye splendid shoulders great depth of heart. Strong quarters even over the back & well rubbed up not showing any of the Irish falling off behind & well let down for galloping—The old mare [22 years?] is quite fresh on her legs & her action unimpaired having been successful last year & now in full training she showed as is quite common with mares of high character a strong spice of Devil & made a charge at me wh had it not been intercepted by the length of her collar shank would inevitably have floored me—The other horses we saw as well as this noble animal Angier drove convinced me

[16]Footnote: "Mr Pierce Butler husband of Fanny Kemble." Butler (1810–1867), a slave-owning Philadelphian outspoken in his support of the Confederacy, had inherited great wealth in Georgia and married actress Fannie Kemble (1809–1893) in 1834. She left him in 1846 and returned to the stage and a successful writing career (*DAB*, X, 315–16; Malcolm Bell, Jr., *Major Butler's Legacy: Five Generations of a Slaveholding Family* [Athens and London, 1987]).

[17]Dr. Alexander Wilcocks (d.1880).

[18]Among the signatures at the back of the diary appears "Wm Rotch Angier of Angier Co Philadelphia," before which Conolly noted Angier's address as 2030 Walnut Street. The city directory lists an "Angier, Hugel & Co. (William Rotch Angier, Adolph Hugel & William G. Allen) malsters and forwarding merchants" (*McElroy's Philadelphia City Directory*, p. 18).

[19]Cornelia (Wadsworth) Ritchie had married Montgomery Ritchie of Boston in 1857. When Conolly met her on the voyage home she was a widow (Hatch, *Wadsworths*, p. 74).

[20]Footnote: "See Invitations [*illegible*]."

[21]It is unclear whether this is the same "Irish beauty" Conolly picked up in the train at Baltimore on 15 April.

that the American horses are first raters as roadsters, far superior to anything we have—We have no idea of the action of an American trotter!

Rained heavily as we returned 3 miles to Phil. & the high action of the black stallion covered us with mud he [don?] the distance in 10 min. & I get in time for an agreeable dinner with Messrs Ward & Col. Campbell[22] to wh I had been specially invited & wh developed the luxuries of this cuisine Terapins being the principal dish, & splendid Chateau Margeaux the drink— Feel much inclined to go to the Peters for the evening but stay at home & smoke & write—

FRIDAY, 21 APRIL

Bk at 9 and up to Mrs Sterrett at 701. Vine St find her all smiles 'Good news' Old Stereotype has sent for her we are to go at once decide upon the 4.30 train. small chat & then off to Peters house where I see Lena Mrs P. Minnie & Miss Wadsworth & stay for 2 hours tell them of my important business call to N. York but promise to come back immediately if not sooner! Goodbye Lena only for a moment! Ill be back & no mistake—Pack up get money for my Tayloe Bill,[23] Buy a hat & some pocket handkfs & order a coach for 3 start for Mrs Sterretts & find her ready up to Station & get tickets &c for N. York & pleasant chat with Mrs Sterrett, tell her in confidence all about Lena—!!!

She is to come to Ireland with St. if it comes off!—pass the Susquehanna by a regular Yankee contrivance the whole train drives aboard a steam barge & is ferried engine & all across & then continues its way to N. York arrive in 4 hours & again steam across the river to the City This time without the cars except that containing the baggage The entire under cover as the steamer backs into a covered shed & we transfer ourselves into the 2 spacious apartments at the sides the cases of Luggage & U.S. mail being run down to the Centre of the barge 5 min & the multitudinous coachmen who have come over to look for fares have all arranged & take the baggage checks & in 10 min. we are landed at the New York Hotel Broadway![24] Supper excellent & bed.

[22]Note among signatures at back of diary: "Mr Campbell, St. Louis—'Irish'—Philadelphia— Ap. 23, 1865."

[23]Footnote: "Tayloe gave me 100 doll Bill or [*illeg.*] for the old horse & buggy at Chatterton."

[24]The New York Hotel, on Broadway from Washington to Waverley Place.

SATURDAY, 22 APRIL

Bk at 8 and out to see Mrs Booth[25] & present my cheque for [*illegible*] 32 find her & little Willy at 54 Waverly Place 3 Avenue. Mr Booth is employed in a Bank & is a very nice fellow—Then to find old Brown[26] No. 90 Beaver St. He tells me Mrs Brown will be glad to see me altho' Old Sterrett informed me she had gone to Canada (aha! I smell a rat!) Fine old cock & true-hearted Southerner! Promised to call on him again. Dr Mackay[27] correspondent of the Times his rooms & find that Lawley has gone to England![28] Read Papers &c. Barnums museum, the Astor House,[29] St Nicholas[30] crowd in the street features of New York. Wall St—Insurance & other companies wonderful go ahead place Find Watson[31] & [Buchan?] & Bill Bushe[32] tog. they oblige me to stay & dine with them. See Mrs Sterrett for a few min: She rallies me about "Lena" Dinner at Delmonico's as good as Paris. Everything in good order among this wonderful Yankee Nation.! Go & drive with Watson & Buchan thro 5th Avenue to the Park! The Park is a great feature & is laid out regardless of cost.[33] Determine to take the owl train at 12 for Philadelphia & arrive

[25]Conolly had first met Mrs. Booth and Willy in Richmond on 23 March.

[26]John Potts Brown, a shipping merchant, was the father of Robert Wells Brown, who, with his wife, Josephine (Lovett) Brown, was involved in Confederate intelligence operations. See entries for 10 March and 2, 5 May.

[27]Charles MacKay (1814–1889), Scottish poet, journalist, and correspondent of the *Times* in New York during the Civil War (*DNB*, XII, 564–65). In his memoirs he recalled being in New York at this time but did not mention Conolly (Charles MacKay, *Forty Years' Recollections of Life . . .* 2 vols. [London, 1877]).

[28]Conolly had seen Lawley off from Richmond on the day the capital fell. Lawley quickly realized he was missing a journalistic opportunity and so turned around at Fredericksburg, witnessed the surrender at Appomattox, journeyed to New York, wrote his last story from America on Lincoln's assassination, and left for England on 18 April, when Conolly was still in Philadelphia (Hoole, *Lawley*, pp. 118–22).

[29]The Astor House Hotel.

[30]The St. Nicholas Hotel, on Broadway at the corner of Spring St.

[31] Among the signatures at the back of the diary, "L. G. Watson" appears twice, once with the names of Richmond acquaintances (see entry for 31 March) and once with those from New York. Like many of Conolly's American acquaintances, Watson was a Briton engaged in the blockade-running business. See *OR*, ser. iv, II, 633–35, 852.

[32]Bushe had accompanied Conolly on the *Owl* from Nassau to the North Carolina coast, but at the last minute, apparently daunted by the journey Conolly proposed to make overland to Richmond, chose a less hazardous route to New York.

[33]Laid out in the 1850s, Central Park had quickly become an important attraction in the life of the city.

When Conolly returned to Philadelphia in the early morning hours of 23 April from a trip to New York City, he found "Large crowd in the Streets waiting to get a view of the Presidents body even at this hour." The body of the slain president lay in state at Independence Hall on that April Sunday. This contemporary print from *Harper's Weekly* depicts the funeral procession for Lincoln a few days later in New York.

at 4 at the Depot 5 at the Hotel Large crowd in the Streets waiting to get a view of the Presidents body even at this hour[34] I go to bed.—

SUNDAY, 23 APRIL

After Bk go out with Harry W. Mr [*illegible*] & Mr Ward Jr to see the R. Catholic Church after SS Peter & Paul[35] just finished, go thro the Bishops House—Find one of the handsomest Italian Churches of finest architecture Corinthian order & correct proportions—a small St Peters. To see the Peters & again in Evg—Two infernal fellows there stay till 11—

MONDAY, 24 APRIL

Mr Kortwright[36] comes to see me & have a long chat about the Fenians Brotherhood![37] Aungier calls & makes an appointment to drive out at 2 Mrs Peters for 10 min. Then Drive over to Suffolk race course 3 miles Mr Angiers two brown mares go a most wonderful pace, I never knew what trotting was before this! He is a capital driver.! The Yankee horse-groom shows his black stallion & indulges in extraordinary obs. By Jesus Christ! An extraordinary character, fearful liar, The Thoroughbred Stallion of 16 hands high & showing much blood. Drive round the track & see what his brown mare really can do it is like flying. The American horse community are even worse than the English of the same kidney—The Race has been put off till Thursday & I shall see it then. Drive home thro beautiful suburbs called W. Philadelphia & Dine with Mr & Mrs Angier in their nice house. She is a very nice woman!—I like her!—Come to England. By all means!—Commodore Turner[38] a red hot Republican comes in & a Lawyer & we have a general chat—! Turner is a renegade South man & is proportionably bitter! I dont think much of him. Je ten fiche pas mal mon brave! Abuse Genl Lee you—you wretchd frog!—Home at 12

[34]The body of the slain president was viewed by Philadelphians at Independence Hall on Sunday, 23 April (*New York Times*, 24 Apr. 1865, p. 8).
[35]The Cathedral Church of St. Peter and St. Paul, Schuylkill Fifth St., between Race and Summer Sts.
[36]Probably Charles E. K. Kortwright, British consul in Philadelphia (*McElroy's Philadelphia City Directory*, p. 538).
[37]The Fenians, or Irish Republican Brotherhood, were a secret society founded in the U.S. in 1858 and dedicated to independence for Ireland. They had underground cells in Ireland, the leaders of which were arrested shortly after Conolly's return from America (R. K. Webb, *Modern England: From the Eighteenth Century to the Present* [New York and Toronto, 1968], pp. 334–35).
[38]Thomas Turner (1808–1883) had commanded the USS *New Ironsides* in the attack on Charleston in April 1863. (*National Cyclopedia of American Biography*, V, 216).

TUESDAY, 25 APRIL

Go with Commodore Turner to the Navy Yard[39] & see Frigate Neeshaminy—3215 tons 2019 [new. reg.?] length 325 feet 4 funnels beam 44—8 boilers 14 guns rifled—Frigate Chattanooga do. &c. &c. &c. 2 funnels 8 boilers—Ironsides 240 feet length 16 guns 58ft 1/2 beam Dalgren 14—11 inch & 2 rifle parrot Monitor Tonawanda 2 funnels 2 fifteen in guns Commodore Turner Philadelphia April 24. 1865.

Then to Mrs Peters & find Lena & her mother then preparing to go to Baltimore for a wedding party. They wont be back till Friday & I go then so here is a go I may return from N. York to see them but heaven knows about the time where I shall be. Things look very fishy for my Love! Go home & dine at 5 order a bottle of champagne to clear my eyes & then go to bed—very seedy—

WEDNESDAY, 26 APRIL[40]

Good bath I begin to look up & cheer up I am in love with Lena & no mistake so here goes, I must go & clear up somewhere & I feel very bad & must get the business straight. so what! Go & see Mrs Peters & if favourable opportunity declare for Lena and make an opportunity to declare to her! Cant bear this suspense!!!! Walk about the street till proper time 12 o'clock thinking I shall probably find her before they start for the accursed wedding at Baltimore train goes at 1.15. Harden my heart & take breath & go for Mrs Peters by Jove I would rather run for Fort Fisher in the hottest of the blockade & yet why I dont know & yet I feel I should like a little danger rather than this suspense—Here goes ring the bell—Pace up & down the room like a tiger in his den for 10 min take up & lay down the books ah here is her sketch half finished Like me I wish to God I was finished Lena!—Here is Miss Wadsworth! looking very handsome that is a [*illegible*] have a small chat with her before Mrs Peters comes & gradually we talk of everything & Lena & we are to go & see Miss Wilcox & then we are to dine at Angiers & we can talk of Lena again & I begin to feel better & I may fix something yet before I leave America & then the boy Willy comes in poor devil he is going to school I read him a small [Essay?]—all for Lena! Lena! Lena! Back to the hotel & take a strong

[39]The ships were the USS *Neshaminy*, not launched until October 1865 and thus apparently under construction at the time of this visit; the USS *Chattanooga*, launched in October 1864 and entered service in May 1866 at Philadelphia; the USS *New Ironsides*, commissioned in 1862 at the Philadelphia Navy Yard; and the USS *Tonawanda*, built at the Philadelphia Navy Yard in 1864 (*ORN*, ser. ii, I, 158, 55, 159, 224).

[40]Conolly misdated this entry 25 April.

corker of cocktail 1.2—& then a good cigar & feel better walking out to Chesnut St meet Kortwright who takes me with his arm & walks me down to his own house—a very pretty French [*illegible*] & then to see Mrs Angier find Angier & Mrs Peters & we go to the horses [*illegible*] till 6 when [*illegible*] home to dress & arrive at [*illegible*] at 6.20 for dinner. dull affair with a buffet Mr & Mrs Kortwright & dull jaw about the war. home 11.30

THURSDAY, 27 APRIL

Went through the town & down to the Delaware & thro all the shipping till 12 o'clock when I returned to the Club to read the papers Thence to meet Angier at the LaPierre & go to witness the trotting race. his beautiful browns take us there in 1/2 an hour & then the sport. The men who carry on the American turf are the roughest lot I ever saw & are decidedly the worst specimens of American society & then the flash betting men jockies & stable hands under them are in all respects as much lower as ours are inferior in grade & more educated in coarse atrocity than their patrons Altogether the personel of an American race-course is "damnable & the Ladies with a good taste & [quietness?] which I have remarked in other things absent themselves entirely from the Races here—The Betting is arranged here in a new way & very easy as there are only 3 or at most 4 horses in a race for instance 1. Hannah Bradley first choice 20 dollars 2. Lennon's Black mare 2nd do. 8— —— 3. One armed Johns do 3—5 ditto In the Pool 33 dollars I took a fancy for one armed John & bought 3 pools averaging 32 dollars on his mare relying solely on the action of the animal The others [*illegible*] heavy favourites at the odds quoted

First heat No 3 went away with the lead but breaking after the first turn never got up again & Lennons bl. mare won by 4 lengths next heat is delayed 20 min. during which the same Auction bidding goes on each better getting a card with No of his pool & the sum paid written on it—Hannah Bradley is still the favourite & in this heat justifies the public choice by winning even altho her long step & very high action dont look like lasting 3rd heat was the most exciting for One armed John went away driving his own mare & began by cutting the other 2 out of the 1st turn a dodge wh is allowed here but does not look well as it had the effect of making Hannah Bradley break as on nearing her he indulged in a superhuman yell this gave him a good start wh he kept all round till the last turn when the 2 others coming up outside the black won by a head there being a dead heat for second same time as before 2m 46 sec for the mile—Great cheering.

4th heat John at his old tactics got again a long lead for the upper corner wh he kept all thro' winning enough 10 lengths—We left then but found he won the other 2 heats & we won our money. 98 dollars—4th heat was the fastest done in 2 min 42 sec—

Flora Temples time over same course was 2 min. 19 sec.—Then home to dine with Angier LaMarquise & Mrs Peters who is looking very well & tres coquette—

Today was a little episode of married life of ["orage"?] which was very lamentable & deprived our dinner of all comfort being more distressing to me & Mrs Peters. LaMarquise who is an exceedingly well dressed piquante Lady entirely a la Française cannot manage her husband who breaks out with atrocious violence carrying all before him!—What a Kettle of Fish about temper She said something about Mrs R—& he fires up. He tells her sister & she feels much annoyed! This will go to Lena & then meanwhile Angier is miserably conscious of being a brute & the poor sensible wife is writhing under the indignity! Really it is great pity to see her thus & he is an unfeeling brute to give her pain no matter what provocation She may give him!—By heavens its horrible If she was led & comforted she would be a nice little woman & attractive withall—home to LaPierre 12

Friday, 28 April

To see the Peters & in Evg to hear the belle of the [faubourg?] at the Arch Theatre—[41]

Saturday, 29 April[42]

Drive out with Angier to see Mr Pierce Butler at his farm Breakfast excellent such butter, such eggs & a cocktail, then to see Mr Potters villa with all its luxuries Fern Rock—Mrs Potter is there small round-about little Lady pretty house—Back to Philad. in a storm of dust. & Dine at the hotel & then to present my violets to Miss Nannie Wadsworth & Mrs Peters. Tea broken in by a Yankee of the name of Cox entirely devoid of manner &c—Curse on him!—Bed—12

[41]Arch Street Theatre, Arch St. above Sixth St.
[42]Footnote: "Drive out with Angier Commodore Turner & Doctor Mason (a regular Cromwellian Englishman."

SUNDAY, 30 APRIL

Dont go to Church—hear from Mrs Sterrett that she has returned & go to her tomorrow—Club—read up English news again to Peters & no girls! God what a nuisance—! I make my frantic declaration to Mrs Peters! She laughs at me They may laugh that win & I will win Lena—the old Lady is evidently against me & the Baltimore dodge has kept the girls out of the way I will talk to Nannie Wadsworth about this Oh it is the Devil! The course of true Love never did run smooth—I will bolt tomorrow![43]

MONDAY, 1 MAY

Very wet morning go round to pay my respects in a very comfortable hack coach Mrs Angier very pleasant all good-nature & good sense That man is a fool! Then to the Consul then to Mrs Sterrett long talk about Sterrett his prospects, Lena & my prospects England & our prospects. Then inevitably to the Peters Miss Wadsworth helps & I call that d——d fellow Cox a brute & back to go to tea on the forlorne hope of seeing the girls! Dine at hotel & Angier comes in & good bye—Out to tea at Peters—No girls damn it damn it damn it—Keep up my [*illegible*] despite the reappearance of that accursed Cox—& be damned to him—Leave them as gaily as circumstances will permit. Start from Philad. at 12 Shunted at New Brunswick to 4 get to New York at 7—Brevoort Ho.[44]—Hot bath after smoking all night with soldiers & Marines! They cant make out what the hell I am—talk French & German to passengers & they cant make me out—

TUESDAY, 2 MAY

Bill how are you!—Take the last berth in the Scotia[45] altho I havt got a cent—go & see old Brown, Delmonico's bar near Wall St The Ladies of Broadway—! Dinner at N. York Hotel after dinner Carnival at the House of a certain [*illegible*]! My excellent quarters & buxome Landlady! Mrs Taylor! nothing can be better—Welly Saunderson[46]—& Baltimore fellow—Bill Bushe Capt North & I—Write to Mrs Peters & send some Music—

---

[43]Marginal note: "dine & spend the day with Pierce Butler Excellent dinner chat with his servant one McManus from Maguires-bridge [a village in Co. Fermanagh] very pleasant party & extreme politics!!! Angier & Butler agree on Matrimony!—Back by 8—."

[44]The Brevoort House Hotel, on Fifth Avenue, corner of Eighth St.

[45]At this point Conolly knew he would be leaving America on 17 May, the day the *Scotia* sailed, thus putting a limit on the time he would have to woo Lena.

[46]For Saunderson, see the last paragraph in the entry for 25 March.

BROADWAY, LOOKING UP FROM EXCHANGE PLACE.

On first seeing New York City, Conolly called it a "wonderful go ahead place," "everything in good order among this wonderful Yankee Nation!" Of Broadway, seen here in an illustration from *Miller's New York As It Is,* he exclaimed "The Ladies of Broadway—!"

WEDNESDAY, 3 MAY

Want of money stress of times! compels me to go to the Consul Mr Archibald[47]—see him & get his promise for £100—see Welly & hear much of Lees last days from Petersburg to Appomattox see Turner from Richmond.[48] ask him to dine Friday Welly Saunderson & I give a dinner at Delmonico's to Bill B. Baltimore chap & North very well done! excellent oysters Chablis 2 soups 2 fish 3 entrees—lamb asparagus champagne 4 bottles—go with Welly to see Mr Angier at the New York Hotel after dinner—cocktails long talk over the last campaign of Richmond & Welly's experience of it—very interesting! Bed 1.30—

THURSDAY, 4 MAY

Lord Newry[49] at the Brevoort[50] chat about Peters excellent Bk & up to Consuls in bus where I found the commander & officers of the Styx[51] from Fortress Monroe come up on a lark—hear the last of Richmond he had gone up there by steamer on the Wed. after it fell—with Consul Archibald to Bank of Messrs Duncan who give me £100 at once—Mrs Duncan is going by "Scotia"—unsuccessful attempt to find Mrs Dort whom I had known a long time ago in a romantic mood in Ireland "Powerscourt[52] & [*illegible*] & the rest of it"—Tired walking the [Pavt?] & come home to go over "The [Fenians?]" till dinner Dine with Newry & Capt Grant from Montreal at Brevoort Ho. Frogs excellent! Chablis coffee ice every Luxury!!! To see Mrs Angier & her pretty

[47]Edward Mortimer Archibald (1810–1884), a colonial official in Newfoundland and British consul-general in New York, 1857–83, knighted in 1882 (*Burke's Landed Gentry* [1921], p. 32). In a vicious obituary, the *New York Times* remembered Conolly's visit to America: "Being in this plight he conceived the idea of blockade running during the war in this country as a means whereby to restore his shattered fortunes, but he miserably failed, and appeared in New-York in a state of utter destitution. Here he was assisted liberally by a gentleman on whom he had no sort of claim, and who had the utmost difficulty in ultimately recovering the money advanced" (*New York Times*, 13 Aug. 1876, p. 6).

[48]Footnote: "No2 his commission for England & signature!!!"

[49]Francis Charles Needham, viscount Newry and Morne (b.1842) (*Burke's Peerage* [1880], p. 696).

[50]Footnote: "Newry's photograph—No10."

[51]HBMS *Styx*, a Royal Navy warship that had been at Hampton Roads on 4 April 1865 (*ORN*, ser. i, XII, 101).

[52]Powerscourt, in County Wicklow, was a grand Palladian country house built not long after Castletown. It survived the Troubles earlier in this century but burned in the 1970s.

sister at the New York Hotel with the old [*illegible*]—meet one of Lees A.D.C. who is deeply depressed with the fall of the South—!![53]

FRIDAY, 5 MAY

Fly around around around Mrs Angier & her sister Mrs Witney[54] go to see Miss Nannie Wadsworth but dont find her so leave message for tomorrow!!—Welly Saunderson gone to the Niagara falls so look up Bill Bushe & old Brown (John Potts) father in law of dear "Mrs Brown" (see Richmond) & with old Turner make a jovial party at Delmonicoes & eat the best dinner I ever saw put on table in an upper chamber where Old Brown comes out strong on his [Minessota?] experiences when the mob 'tried it on with him' the first year of the war because his son had exulted in the "Battle of Bulls run" when asked by a ruffian for his opinions he said, on what subject? What I have had for Breakfast or what, no your opinions on the country! Waal you know what a pidgeon is? Yes hes a middling smart bird? Yes, Waal I guess it will take a Pidgeon a mighty short time to fly a distance! Why yes certainly well it will take a Pidgeon to fly from here to Hell & back again before I tell you my opinion so now make the most o' that!!!! We broke up about 10. & I went down to see La Marquise & her sister & arranged to take them to the Theatre tomorrow!—

SATURDAY, 6 MAY

Bk at Brevoort. very wet morning hire a coach & go to see Miss Nannie Wadsworth & am received with great courtesy by her mother[55] & herself very fine house abounding in works of art & paintings of merit & beautiful pictures of high bred cattle all numbered from the Geneseo stud book—Picture of the large trees & spreading parks of Geneseo which must be a Paradise on Earth I believe the finest country residence in all America—& such Ladies—The Old Lady magnificent Nannie, a beautiful type of the handsome race & Mrs Richie whose picture only I saw as she was not well more superb than either Lady this country can produce fine women & no mistake & I

[53]Conolly does not identify this officer. It was not C. M. Wilcox, who had accompanied Conolly from Raleigh to Richmond and wrote in 1877, "I was in New York ten days after the surrender, on my way to Texas, a paroled prisoner; met Conley the first night. He gave an amusing account of his leaving Richmond in the night and his difficulties in reaching the Baltimore and Ohio railroad. He urged me to go to Ireland with him, and supposing I wanted money, offered me his purse freely" (*SHSP*, IV, 22n.).

[54]Footnote: "Mrs Witney is a very great beauty with an acquiline nose & fine eyes & a lazy insouciante manner of lovely indolence wh is charming."

[55]Mary Craig Wharton of Philadelphia, wife of slain Union general James S. Wadsworth.

believe everything else in perfection!!!! We had a long chat the burden of which was of course "Lena" incomparable Lena & she consents to give me despatches for 'Lena' tomorrow when I repair once more to Philadelphia to do or die—stay there an hour & a half when the old Lady offers me her pew in Church & Nannie tells me to go & see her after church so I know what to do—I swear eternal friendship & nothing more for Nannie & go in heart & soul for "Lena" incomparable "Lena' Raining hard so devote day to business & Bill Bushe so go with him about the town in my coach first to Brewsters where I order 2 American carriages,[56] then to Dr Mackay the plucky old correspondent of "the Times" Then to buy Rifles revolvers &c at 177—Broadway!!!! (vide invoice)[57] Back to my comfortable home at Mrs Taylors in 9th St & had hardly lighted my pipe when in comes Duncan the Banker to ask me to join his party at *"Delmonico"* same Ladies &c—pleasant chat—but sorry to refuse as I dine with B. B. & go to the Theatre with LaMarquise & Mrs Witney

The play "The Black Sheep" at Wallacks Theatre[58] The two Ladies B. B & I[59]—Excellent capital acting & famous plot Farce Comedy!!!—Supper at The New York Hotel & Bed at 2

SUNDAY, 7 MAY

Go to Ch at Grace Church[60] & am shown by the fat usher to Mrs Wadsworths pew all very handsome a new gothic Church with glass painted windows & [walnut?] fittings everything orthodox & very well conducted partic the music wh was beautiful in fact all the characteristics of wealthy devotion—Mss Nannie in crepe (very black) next me & Mr & Mrs Duncan hard by & the whole congregation of same type.! Back with Miss Wadsworth & a long chat during which in the most arch manner she hands me *"her despatches"* for Lena—telling me that I was to [see?] them!! What can she mean she knows all my declaration to Mrs Peters &c & the object of my visit now!!—Dine with the Marquise & her sister & old [*illegible*] (Mrs [*illegible*] father) & fine old Dame! with most courteous manners—I had called at Mrs Duncans' & was kindly & graciously admitted by pretty Mrs Duncan! who made herself very agreeable! Then take the Marquise & Mrs Witney & drove

---

[56]Footnote: "vide invoice No12 New Appx." In *Miller's New York As It Is, or Stranger's Guide-Book*. . (New York, 1871) appeared an advertisement for Brewster & Co.: "Elegant Carriages & Road Wagons in the newest Designs" (opposite p. 82).

[57]Footnote: "invoice of firearms bought in New York Cooper & Pond."

[58]Wallacks Theatre, corner of Broadway and Thirteenth St.

[59]Footnote: "Best actress (Miss Henriques—)"

[60]Grace Episcopal Church, Broadway near Tenth St.

in the Park. bid goodbye we shall meet at Philad I am to start tomorrow morg. *Smoke a pipe* with B. B & we go over our mutual plans I tell him vaguely about Lena—

MONDAY, 8 MAY

Start by the 10 o'clock train & arrive at Philadelphia at 1/2 past 1 capital run & very pleasant companions 2 ladies from Jersey City[61] who beg me to go & see them & an Irish girl in the Ferry boat[62] admire the high cultivation & beautiful villas along the line of Railway to New Brunswick where my fair friends leave me! And I have to make the best of "the balance" consisting of the conductors wife a good natured Yank Lady with lots of talk. The conductor a very jolly fellow points out the parts of the country Trenton 'the Delaware' here the country houses are of a most luxurious character & the places kept in the highest order for 25 miles to Philad.—Arrive & jump into a coach for the LaPierre & before 2 find Lena & Minnie & stay with them in great happiness till 4 when I go & take off my jack books & put on evg clothes & back again at 5 when we have a rehearsal of "La Diplomatie de marriage" a pretty little piece from the Follies [*illegible*] in wh both the charming girls act with the obnoxious Cox. Lena is a little frightened & pouts. Minnie very amiable & serious!! They were like all amateurs much too rapid in articulation!! Some ice cream & then away to dine with Angier truly I am a lucky dog born under a lucky Star everything turns out well! In comes Mrs Angier & an awful cold meeting—! Thats shocking—He never rises or says a word— damned bad! I sit with her the whole evening pleasant chat she is a very pleasant high-sould woman & determined not to be bullied! It is dreadful to see her so trampled on & such high spirited resistance!—

Walk home with the little Sicilian singing master who chatters all the time about Palermo & the fortune he has made here 20,000 dollars from 500 wh he began with & now he has his country place where he receives all the Italian Ship Captains & his [*illegible*] his musical classes & his pupils during the season & his wife & children ah signor Questa paese superbo, magnifica!!!!— Another glass of brandy cocktail & bona notte!!!!!! [*illegible*] in Ingelterra!!

---

[61]Footnote: "Miss Davis—126 York St. Jersey City."
[62]Footnote: "Margaret Kennan 45 West Street near Landing Wharf."

CHAPTER SIX

THE VOYAGE HOME

[Without explanation, Conolly neglected his diary for more than a week. Apparently his last meeting with Lena was the cause. Not even the fall of Richmond had that effect on him. The diary begins again when Conolly copied out a letter he received from Nannie Thomas in Richmond.]

Write out Nannie Thomas letter & my answer & inclosure to Genl Lee

Ballard House Richmond April 27. 1865

("Nannie Thomas' letter")

Mr Conolly

I received only yesterday your letter[1] & hasten to let you know of our existence—All of these terrible events crowding together in such rapid succession have rendered me physically & mentally totally incompetent for letter-writing but I will try & tell you what I have been doing & what we have suffered since those horrid Yankees came into our City. Our Soldiers you know fired a warehouse on Cary St filled with Tobacco, the wind being high the flames spread & by three o'clock in the afternoon all the business portion of the city was burnt. The scene was terrific the Yankees advancing on & the whole city apparently in flames It reminded me of the burning of Moscow The enemy much to the surprize of everyone have behaved very well here no signs of exultation or taunting spirit have they exhibited but with the surrender of Lee's army I have lost my spirits and I hate to write it in my hope for the Cause What a dark picture! What a terrible future our noble old Virginia in chains & governed by Yankees is it not galling & terrible! I wish with you that my Father & family could leave this country & go to England but to

---

[1]Given the uncertainty of the mails in the turmoil following Richmond's fall, if she received his letter on 26 April, he must have written her very soon after he reached Philadelphia on 17 April.

116

carry on our Confederate Government Papa invested largely in Confederate bonds & stock which are now only so much paper—.[2] I went a few days ago to see Genl Lee,[3] poor man he is so much depressed we have none of us the means, no matter how strong the inclination to leave this country & we will have to go to work—We owned a great many slaves but now they have all left us Papa purchased a great many not long since & has of course lost all that—I dont mind being poor, I can learn to wait on myself & to do with little but to loose my country is to me the most terrible blow that could befall me—I go out very little, I have only been in the street three times since the Yankees came I have talked with several Yankees & treated them with studied indifference & Dignity. Never can I forget the noble friends of mine who have fallen by their foul hands They are very much enraged by the Death of their President It will do us no good We have nothing to expect from Andy Johnston[4] the low Plebeian who rules over us now! I am very angry with England France & the whole European world Why did they not help the noble Confederates, that a gallant resistance against such fearful odds. this war has been comparatively a skeleton fighting against a giant. When I see their vast resources I think theirs is the side that merits reproach that they did not destroy our noble but small armies long 'ere this. I must change the subject for I will get so excited I can never stop—I have lost many friends in the late battles Our mutual friend General Geary[5] would not surrender but has made his way to Johnstone—I saw this morning Colonel Manning[6] of Longstreets staff He expects to go to Brazil very soon Genl Longstreet takes it very seriously & is particularly sad—I hope our President may make his escape[7] He knows his Life is at stake & will I suppose make time—you will take my good wishes, & thanks for your kindnesses & sympathy back across the waters with you & remember if ever you get into a war with the United States the hearts of the Confederate Ladies will be with you as well as the swords of our men—I have drawn quite a long draught on your Patience Ma, my sisters & brother send their kindest regards We have not

[2]Her father, Henry Wirtz Thomas, managed to pick up the pieces and, in 1875, become lieutenant governor of Virginia.

[3]After Appomattox Lee lived briefly at 707 E. Franklin St. in the house his family had rented for much of the war. The Lee House, as it became known, later served as headquarters for the Virginia Historical Society for many years.

[4]A Union man from Tennessee, Andrew Johnson (1808–1875) was held in special contempt by unreconstructed southerners.

[5]Conolly had met Brig. Gen. Martin W. Gary on 21 March in Richmond. Here he misspells Gary's name again.

[6]Col. Peyton T. Manning had served on Longstreet's staff since 1861 (*CSO*, p. 124).

[7]Jefferson Davis was not captured until 10 May.

heard yet from our brother who is with Mosby. but trust that he is safe! He is with Mosby who has not yet surrendered. He will hold out to the last.[8] Upon your return home it will be very easy for you to communicate with me & I will be very happy always delighted to hear from you. When I commenced I had no idea of writing so much this has gotten to be quite a ragged letter on so many different scraps of paper Ma sends her kind regards & some messages which I have not time to write or space—I fear I have already tired you.—Write me a long letter on receipt of this

Good bye Your True & distressed Friend

— Nannie—

Mr Thomas Conolly Brevoort House New York

Answer[9]

On board 'Scotia' New York bound for Liverpool May 17th 1865[10]

My dearest Miss Nannie

I have just returned here after a visit to Philadelphia[11] I enclose a letter for Genl Lee wh you will be kind enough to deliver with your own true hand—I leave it open so that you can read it—I will send you some money as soon as I get to England as I know your fearful want of Everything My dearest Girl I hope you are now a little calm & tranquil after the long agony you have had. I will be in Richmond I hope by November next[12] & you will I know write to me to London & keep me posted on all events concerning the dear heroic South—Dearest Miss Nannie the day will come 'ere long when the South will certainly establish her own So much heroic blood was never spilt in vain!

---

[8]Mosby disbanded the 43d Battalion Partisan Rangers on 21 April. Nannie evidently did not know this when she wrote Conolly six days later.

[9]Marginal note: "To Miss Nannie Thomas."

[10]Conolly had crossed out the original heading: "Brevoort Ho. New York May 9th 1865."

[11]Crossed through: "Niagara & Canada." It is unclear whether Conolly visited, or only planned to visit, the Niagara Falls area in the time for which there is a gap in his diary. He was in the vicinity of New York City for part of that time, for at the back of the diary is a notation similar to the one he used in his London diaries to record assignations with prostitutes: "Minnie W. Kay Staten Island—May 13. 1865."

[12]There is no reference in any of Conolly's papers to this idea of returning to Virginia and no evidence that he ever did.

Let me know how Genl Lee is looking & how he bears his unexampled lot—![13] And in the Fall as it is then quite quiet The bustle of affairs only lasting 6 months, the remaining six months quite tranquil—

You require rest & quiet & do my dear Friend allow me the deep & heartfelt gratification of ministering it to you—

May God Almighty bless & keep you in his Holy hand & may His good Providence ever rule for good the lot of the magnanimous South.

General, dear & honored Friend I bid you Adieu Saunderson[14] joins me in his best Duty & Affection to you!

Yrs Truly Thomas Conolly

Genl Robert E. Lee

&c &c &c

WEDNESDAY, 17 MAY

10 Received on board Passengers & baggage—[15] 10.45 the Mails—Backed out of Dock Left New York at full speed Noon moderate & clear passed Staten Island Light Ho—passed Sandy Hook discharged the Pilot The Light Ship abeam Set all sail Fire Island Light Ho abeam. Passed American Ship "Republic" bound W. Moderate & clear with heavy Lightn'g to the N. Midnight Light winds. In all sail Average speed 13 K—Course—E. 1/2 S—wind variable—[16]

THURSDAY, 18 MAY

Up at 430 Got a glorious Bath from hose & went on deck, very cold & occasional fog ship swinging along. cup of Coffee from Quarter Master.

[13]A page is missing on which Conolly ended his letter to Nannie Thomas and began the one to Lee.

[14]Conolly mentioned Saunderson because he had fought with Lee's cavalry during the retreat from Petersburg to Appomattox. Conolly never indicated whether he knew if Saunderson had met Lee, but this reference implies as much.

[15]"Thos. Connelly, M.P., England" appears on a passenger list for the *Scotia*, bound for Liverpool. During the voyage Conolly mentioned the names of several of the more than two hundred fifty others listed but apparently did not take notice of "Mr. A. Carnegie, Pittsburgh" (*New York Times*, 18 May 1865, p. 8 [hereafter cited as "passenger list"]).

[16]A chart of wind direction, course, and barometric pressure by hour follows.

Bk at 8.30.—write up Log—Play with Children Sopia Duncan[17] & [Alek?]—Arthur & Jack Wadsworth. Look after Mrs Ritchie[18]—Wind arises write up Journal smoke, & read. Tend the Ladies on deck all day—Ship goes magnificently hardly any motion—A very pleasant dinner now that we are beginning to know one-another & all seem to wish to make themselves pleasant—To bed early.

FRIDAY, 19 MAY

Up at 6. too late for Bath. Write up Log. smoke & Bk—
Children's play "Jessy Duncan" with her poke bonnet & old Lady ways— The two small Ritchies like 2 Java sparrows, Look after Mrs Ritchie & the Ladies Mrs Belmont[19] Mrs Duncan &c &c Dinner very merry Tea on Deck with Mrs Ritchie confess my Love & last scene with "Lena"

SATURDAY, 20 MAY

Up at 3.30—Bath by Hose.!—Coffee fair wind. Bk with little princess— read [*illegible*] Write up Log. Take care of Mrs Ritchie. Dinner pleasant After dinner on deck with Mrs Ritchie [*illegible*] with her—[*illegible*] bed.[20]

"Cornelia W. Ritchie"

A lovely woman in the very prime & pride of her woman-hood, Still wearing mourning for her husband fashionable & worthy daughter of the most distingué Lady I ever saw & Genl Wadsworth a noble soldier killed at the battle of the Wilderness "She walks in beauty" above the ordinary size with a superb goddess-like figure of the most easy graceful lines & a well set-on head—Her dark hair in great profusion crowns a noble brow the whole of whose contour recalls the idea of the Noble Roman Lady whose historic name she bears. Calm pale & lighted up with a luminous intelligence such a head is born to command! And bear its soft empire to a widespread circle— Add to her majestic beauty the kind genial manner & sweet smile which is peculiarly her own & see her playing with her darling little boys you have the most striking group that sculptor ever studied or Man desired to call "his own" She has suffered considerable illness partly from the climate of

[17]Wife of the banker Conolly met in New York, "Mrs. W. B. Duncan, three children, two servants" ("passenger list").
[18]"Mrs. Ritchie, two children and servant" ("passenger list"). Conolly had met Cornelia (Wadsworth) Ritchie's sister, Nannie, at the Peters' house in Philadelphia on 18 April and knew of Cornelia, though it is unclear whether he had met her before boarding the *Scotia*.
[19]"Mrs. Belmont and servant, New-York" ("passenger list").
[20]A chart of wind direction, course, and barometric pressure by hour follows.

America & its severe action upon the nervous system as all her family & herself had & her [*illegible*] into the deepest affliction by the death of her father & then of her husband. And a serious illness followed when she was advised total change of scene & climate for 2 years—Her beauty is rather enhanced by her pale delicate complexion which is in turn set off by her rich [*illegible*] exquisitely pencilled dark eye brows & rich hazel eyes—Truly Mrs Ritchie is a noble woman & as amiable as she is noble combining the simplicity of the Roman Lady with the ease & elegance of the 19th century—The leader of high-caste Americans, the favorite of the Town of New York, the belle of Newport, the best-dressed most fashionable, charming coquetteish beauty of the petite Contesse school is a distinguished ornament to our "Scotia." She is evidently accustomed to be attended & caressed & her little languid ways gently suggesting attention & assistance are part of the character of Leader of the brilliant Ladies of New York which she has played with admirable success & ever-increasing popularity for some time—Owner of a beautiful house in the 5th Avenue which is like its mistress Perfection in all its appointments & with graceful winning manners & a large & hospitable kindness it is no wonder that such a Lady should be easily installed in the Leadership of those who are [*illegible*] more in their quickness & versatility of observation & proverbially devoted to their Lovely Ladies—

SUNDAY, 21 MAY

Up at 4 Bathe by hose. raining hard. so retire to bed again till 7 Still raining & very foggy—

Passed an Ice berg which created great sensation everybody rushing on deck to see it & beautiful it was. an irregular pile of pure white snow with aqua-marine veins of purest color making the water all around the most lovely blue it wafted by in from the thick fog not more than 50 yds distance & could be seen some time as the sun emerged simultaneously & the fog rose—

Church in the Grand saloon all Passengers 288 attend Seamen in the [after port?] near [Binnacle?] Capt Judkins[21] reads Prayers & leads the 100th Psalm & then reads Sermon "Were there not 10 cleansed but where are the nine There is not to give glory to God save this Stranger" [*illegible*] the prayers for this safe voyage &c as prescribed in the Prayer Book—Dinner 4—Cap-

---

[21]Notice under ships cleared in the "Marine News" column, New York *World*, 19 May 1865: "Steamship Scotia, Judkins, Liverpool—E Cunard." Later Conolly made the marginal notation: "Log of the S. S. 'Scotia' Capt. C. H. E. Judkins."

tains Cabin with Ladies afterwards Mrs Ritchie Mrs Duncan Mrs Belmont bed. 11.

MONDAY, 22 MAY

Bathe by hose at 3.45. Then read the war story till 8.30. Then Mrs Ritchie & other Ladies [*illegible*] on deck till dinner. Driven in by rain supper Toddy & bed

TUESDAY, 23 MAY

Bathe by hose 4—Coffee &c. Read & write Journal—Smoke—Miss Fanny Hill[22] begins to create a sensation—Pleasant Dinner. On deck till 11 with Mrs Ritchie—

WEDNESDAY, 24 MAY

Queens Birth day I propose the health of Victoria Queen of England. Mr Blogett[23] proposes [*illegible*] President of U.S. sing "God Save the Queen" And "The Star Spangled Banner" Supper on deck Mrs Ritchie & Mrs Belmont—Bed. 11.30. All's well TC[24]

THURSDAY, 25 MAY

Bath at 4.30. Read up Extracts of official reports ("Army & Navy (American) Journal") of Battles of the Campaign from [*illegible*] Bentonville fort Steadman, Hatchers Run, five forks, Petersburg, Farmville, & Appomattox. Reports very fair & give every credit to Southern arms. Sleeping & smoking & eating 'till Ladies appear about 1.—

Then squire them as usual Dinner Turtle soup. last dinner but one & Supper & write to Mrs Peters in anticipation of Queenstown tomorrow. Make Fastness Light[25] at 11.30. p.m.[26]

---

[22]At first glance, this appears to be a reference to John Cleland's *Fanny Hill, or the Memoirs of a Woman of Pleasure* (1750), certainly an appropriate book for someone of Conolly's inclinations. There was, however, an entry in the *Scotia*'s passenger list for "Miss Fanny Hill, Boston" ("passenger list").

[23]"Mr. and Mrs. W. T. Blogett, New-York" ("passenger list").

[24]There follows a chart giving wind direction, course, and barometric pressure, the text of part of the poem, "Barbara Fritchie," and another chart.

[25]Fastnet Lighthouse, built on a rock off the coast of Co. Cork.

[26]There follows another chart of wind direction, course, and barometric pressure.

FRIDAY, 26 MAY

Up at 3 by order of the Hose-bearer capital immersion last Bath of the Scotia & when dressed see old Kinsale Head[27] about 10 miles to E. make Queenstown by 5. and discharges mails[28] & passengers & proceed on our Voyage with a Liverpool Pilot, our dear old Capt who had been up all night retires to his den to have a good sleep part with Clara Smith,[29] and Annie & Bessie Fitch,[30] Ella Garrett[31] & her mother of Baltimore & her friend Helen Stuart[32] who have been very pleasant during the voyage take affectionate adieu of Mr Watson[33] who has cultivated her during his [*illegible*]. Ella is a pretty budding little blonde very ready & willing to be loved & all the charm & sangfroid of America which strikes us stuck up people so much.[34]

[27]Old Head of Kinsale, a cape near the entrance to Kinsale Harbor, south Co. Cork.

[28]On this day the U.S. consul in Liverpool, who had been following Conolly's travels, wrote to Washington: "The Telegrams from Queenstown this morning bring us the news of the capture of Jefferson Davis. I do not know what the effect of this will be in other parts of England, but here it has extinguished the last ray of hope for the Rebellion" (U.S. consul, Liverpool, 26 May 1865, T141, NA).

[29]Signature at back of diary: "Clara Smith. New York." Passenger list: "Miss Clara Smith, Miss Jones, Mr. and Mrs. W. A. Smith, N.Y."

[30]Signatures at back of diary: "Annie Fitch Bessy Fitch New York." Passenger list: "Mrs. Fitch and two daughters, New-York."

[31]Signature at back of diary: "Ella G. Garrett 508 W. Fayette St. Baltimore Md."

[32]Signature at back of diary: "Helen M. Stuart 242 N. Calvert St. Baltimore Md." Passenger list: "Miss Helen Stuart, Baltimore."

[33]Probably "John L. S. Watson, England" ("passenger list").

[34]Another chart of statistics follows.

EPILOG

The voyage over, Tom Conolly ended his diary and returned home, eager to tell friends of his adventure abroad. It takes little effort to imagine his sending the members of his London clubs scurrying for cover to avoid yet another tale of the last days of the Confederacy. His stories were not anything like those he had imagined before leaving Ireland the previous November, however. Certainly they did not have the endings he had anticipated then. His and his partners' hopes for the *Emily* had been dashed by the storm at sea and then by the success of northern arms at Fort Fisher. The cause he admired and sought to aid had turned to ashes literally before his eyes. And he had failed in love.

Conolly nevertheless did not let any of these disappointments trouble him for very long. Although a hard look at his bank balance would have suggested greater caution, he seems to have dismissed his participation in the enterprise of the *Emily* as just another minor bad investment. Because he was not a southerner, he could not have felt the bitterness and self-reproach that prostrated many partisans of the cause now lost. And within days of being rejected by Lena Peters he was charming the women on board the ship bound for home. At most, a few years later he might have been reminded of his romantic defeat in America when an Irish landowner well known to him married Cornelia Wadsworth Ritchie[1]—with whom he had flirted on the *Scotia* and whose brother eventually won the hand of Lena Peters.

It is hard to read Conolly's diary without concluding that the author did not fully appreciate the risks and dangers that had filled his travels. Through-

---

[1] She married John George Adair, a wealthy landlord and justice of the peace in the same two Irish counties as Conolly, Kildare and Donegal. Adair bought the County Donegal estate of Glenveagh from the earl of Leitrim in 1870 and built a Gothic-style castle there. His American wife became famous as a hostess in Ascendancy society (Guinness and Ryan, *Irish Houses & Castles*, p. 85). Conolly could easily have been among her guests on occasion, perhaps even when her sister-in-law visited from across the water.

out the six months he was away from Britain, from the time a storm crippled the *Emily* during the first week of the voyage to the day the *Scotia* nearly rammed an iceberg on the return trip, Tom Conolly had had his share of close calls. Reaching the North Carolina coast—without incident, on the last blockade runner, after the closing of the last port—required extraordinary luck. Giving hardly a thought to this good fortune, he then managed to avoid the northern army that had just taken Wilmington, walk inland through miles of pine barrens and swamps, and leave Fayetteville only days before it too passed from southern hands.

Once he reached Raleigh, he was temporarily out of harm's way, as was true of his time in Richmond. The same could not be said, though, about being under fire with Lee in the opening scenes of the last campaign in Virginia. With the fall of Richmond, Conolly's luck held long enough to see the M.P. out of town. Fortunately for him, he fell in with a traveling companion who knew the route northward and could provide shelter when they reached the Potomac. Crossing into Maryland penniless, no longer the free-spending foreign celebrity he had been in Richmond, Conolly should have been thankful that his passage down the river and up the Chesapeake Bay as a deckhand on a suspicious vessel ended without mishap. From Baltimore onward, his travels had no more remarkable or dangerous aspect than those of other wealthy Britons visiting America. To get to that point, however, Conolly surely put the luck of the Irish to a stern test.

His travels were equally noteworthy for his repeated if unwitting association with some of the sharpest characters of the Confederacy. As an unsuccessful investor in the southern war effort, throughout his journey Conolly was nearly always in the company of a fellow traveler, if not a principal agent, in either blockade running or espionage. Given the nature of his investment, he naturally had dealings with Americans and Britons involved in transactions of questionable legality. When he decided, however, not merely to invest but also to accompany his investment to America, he put his life as well as his money in the hands of a class of men hitherto unknown to him.

The first step in this unaccustomed association was taken even before he set foot on the deck of the *Emily*, when Conolly joined the partnership of John Palliser and other respectable British gentlemen. If Palliser was only a dabbler in blockade running, as seems to have been the case, others, in particular Robert McDowell, were not so inexperienced. And the farther the M.P. ventured from the safe, familiar society of the landed gentry—those same sleek and contented men he professed to scorn when in fact he was as representative of their type as anyone—the more he came into contact with shadier, less genteel characters who were unimpressed with the rituals and ranks of polite society. When Conolly threw in his lot with the notorious Maffitt on his last run to the Carolina coast, in the company of the gun runner Sterrett, he put himself among some very hard men indeed.

It is not surprising that in the company of blockade-running merchants Conolly would rub shoulders with Confederate spies. What is striking is the number of the latter fraternity that he met during his brief travels through the South. The initial contact seems to have been Sterrett, who accompanied Conolly to the southern capital and later left with Josephine Brown, a veteran courier in the Confederate intelligence network. It would seem that Sterrett introduced Conolly and. Brown. Certainly the three of them spent much of their time in Richmond together. From that first meeting with Brown until he left Virginia, Conolly was rarely out of sight of someone associated with southern espionage. This close contact was probably assured very early during his month in the capital when he met the sinister genius of the Confederate intelligence service and head spymaster himself, Major William Norris.

Even John Tayloe, Conolly's fellow refugee from burning Richmond, was not simply another fleeing Confederate officer cut off from his regiment. He too was no stranger to espionage and put Conolly in touch with that colorful desperado, Thomas Nelson Conrad, one of the most successful rebel spies. The M.P. could not be faulted for failing to see at the time how lucky he was not to have been in Conrad's company too long. If he had been with that sharp character one week later—when the spy was arrested on suspicion of being John Wilkes Booth, who had fled after shooting Lincoln into Conrad's private theater of operations on the Potomac—there could have been an unpleasant diplomatic incident involving the master of Castletown. The next contact, Captain Spaulding of the schooner *Abeona*, was himself no innocent, having been under suspicion by Federal authorities throughout the war for engaging in clandestine trade between Maryland and Virginia. All in all, after sailing with Spaulding's lot Conolly was fortunate to arrive in Baltimore with no greater injury than the calluses he had acquired from a little unwonted manual labor.

The connection with southern espionage did not end with Conolly's escape from the war zone and return to orderly society, for the M.P. again fell in with Sterrett and Josephine Brown's father-in-law in New York. He knew something of the suspicious activities of all of these southern acquaintances, but his diary hardly gave them their due as participants in the desperate schemes that brought sustenance and intelligence into the Confederacy through the seaborne blockade and overland through contested territory.

If he had little inkling of the activities of the Confederate spies he met, Conolly was completely unaware that he himself had become the object of intense diplomatic attention. The *Emily* had not escaped the notice of the United States consuls in Glasgow and Cardiff, who in December 1864 dutifully reported the ship to Washington as a suspected blockade runner. Liverpool consul Thomas H. Dudley took a special interest in Conolly even before knowing his name, having read within days of the *Emily*'s sailing a newspaper account about the preparations of a wealthy but unnamed M.P. to run the blockade. Not until much later, in March 1865, did he piece together enough evidence to identify Conolly as the unnamed parliamentarian and to learn that he had not been captured and thrown into a Federal prison, as had been rumored.[2]

The next diplomatic report on Conolly came to Washington after Captain Maffitt reached Cuba following his last dash to the coast of the mainland. The American consul general in Havana wrote his superiors that "the steamer 'Owl' had recently gone to the Coast of North Carolina and landed there among other passengers an Irish member of the British Parliament whose name is not given, carrying important despatches to the Insurgents."[3] Despite the national preoccupation with the great events of that spring—Sherman's progress of destruction through the Carolinas and Grant's preparations for a final offensive in Virginia—the intelligence from Havana set the State Department's antennas aquiver. In response to the department's request that he investigate the matter, the Liverpool consul confirmed "after much enquiry" that the unnamed, blockade-running M.P. was Tom Conolly. Dudley also determined that Conolly had arrived safely in Richmond but could not decide among conflicting reports whether his ship ever reached a southern port or whether the M.P. carried any dispatches for the Confederate government. There the investigation rested until Dudley concluded it with a report to Washington a week after the *Scotia* reached Liverpool that Conolly had returned to Britain.[4]

It is likely that the *Owl* did carry dispatches on that last voyage to North Carolina. The American consuls in Nassau and Havana believed so. The southern commissioner in England had continued to send messages after all ports were closed in hopes that couriers could somehow reach the mainland from the Bahamas by unconventional means.[5] And it is unlikely that Maffitt—

[2]U.S. consul, Liverpool, 14 Dec. 1864, 22 Mar. 1865, T141, NA.

[3]Ibid., 11 May 1865. The quotation is Dudley's paraphrase of the Havana report.

[4]Ibid., 11 May, 2 June 1865.

[5]Virginia Mason, ed., *The Public Life and Diplomatic Correspondence of James M. Mason*... (New York and Washington, D.C., 1906), pp. 540–41.

who knew in advance there would be no opportunity to offload cargo—would have risked his ship merely to ferry a few private passengers to the Carolina shore when he had decided to head instead for Havana and then Galveston. At all events, if there were dispatches they must have been delivered, for Conolly and the other passengers reached Richmond in due course.[6] At that late date in the war, however, the content of the messages and their value for the southern cause can hardly have been worth the effort Maffitt and others had devoted to their safe delivery.

Conolly saw the Confederacy at its bitter end, but what did he see? As a foreigner who knew no more about the South than he had read in the distorted British newspaper accounts of the war, he did not start his journey from an especially well-informed perspective. And as a prominent foreigner with gold in his pocket and a penchant for fast living, he did not seek to observe daily life among ordinary southerners. Despite these handicaps, Conolly managed quite well to record the last days of the Confederacy.

The manner of his arrival and of his escape from Richmond brought him into touch not only with the elite but also with the humblest southerners. Even if he did not seek out such acquaintances, he nevertheless did not fail to describe them, their circumstances, and their opinions. He naturally wrote the most about the leading figures he met—in particular the haggard president and the idolized general. Though stereotyped in their effusive prose, even these sketches enlarge the surviving record on the Confederate elite on the eve of defeat.

Even Conolly's love of good food and drink add to our understanding of life in the Confederacy, both in fashionable homes in the capital and in farmhouses in the countryside. Discounting the desire of his hosts to appear at their best, it is still apparent from Conolly's account that the larders of the well-to-do in Richmond were not yet completely bare. Even in more modest homes the visitor from Ireland did not seem to lack for plentiful and varied, if plain, food.

The journey from the reading room of his London club to the reality of Lee's Petersburg camp did little to dampen the visitor's optimism for southern victory. Much of this lack of realism can be laid to Conolly's naiveté, though there were southerners too who still hoped the unrelieved string of military reverses might yet miraculously be made right. Moreover, the natural desire of his hosts to impress him did nothing to disabuse the M.P. of his rosy assessment. No episode better reveals the classic problem of the outsider seeking to understand a strange environment than Conolly's Potemkin

---

[6]Interestingly, Conolly's first call in Richmond, the same day he checked into his hotel, was on Mrs. James Murray Mason, wife of the Confederate commissioner in London.

visit to the fleet at Drewry's Bluff. To his foreigner's eyes the fleet seemed to be a powerful asset in the arsenal of the Confederacy. The admiral in command, however, knew as he glibly told Conolly the South would yet fight it out to victory that the truth was not one of resolute defiance but of mass desertion and loss of the will to win. In such circumstances, a more perceptive visitor than Conolly might have been lulled into doubting the chances for northern victory. Conolly, however, should at least have sensed that the Confederate forces he visited were marking time, waiting to respond to the enemy's movements. If he had thought much about the circumstances, seeing that all initiative had passed to the other side, he would not have been so blithely optimistic.

The diary records Conolly's observations on America, but what kind of impression did he make on Americans? Certainly those northerners like Dudley, who followed Conolly's travels at a distance, shared a low opinion of the M.P. The Liverpool consul complained in his first report on Conolly's preparations to sail, without knowing his identity, that "he is not the first member of Parliament who has been engaged in this business. There is no class of society in England exempt, from the highest and most refined to the lowest and most degraded. Members of Parliament, Mayors, Magistrates, Alderman, Merchants and Gentlemen are all alike daily violating the law of Nations."[7] Later Dudley wrote bitterly of the lives lost because Conolly and like-minded Britons chose to aid the South. More generally, according to the *New York Times* Conolly was of that class "of Irish gentry whose aim in life seems to be to prove how they can best abuse the good gifts of fortune. . . . a type of that class, happily becoming rare, which more than anything else conduced to make Ireland the scene of misery" earlier in the century.[8]

These comments were made by people who had not met the M.P. and were in any case hardly in sympathy with his reasons for visiting America. What of those he did meet? Several Confederate officers mentioned Conolly in their memoirs and diaries. Some remembered him warmly; others merely noted his presence. Major General Cadmus M. Wilcox, who escorted the visitor from North Carolina to Richmond, described him as "this genial and warm-hearted stranger" who "was eccentric in the dress he wore on the streets and about camp" and "had all the vivacity, and much of the wit and humor peculiar to his race."[9] Captivated by a long talk with the M.P. as he

[7]U.S. consul, Liverpool, 14 Dec. 1864, NA.

[8]*New York Times*, 13 Aug. 1876. This passage from an obituary notice was written by someone who remembered Conolly's visit to New York after running the blockade but who took up most of the space with a general indictment of the landlords of Ireland.

[9]*SHSP*, IV, 21n–22n.

escorted him around the battlefield at Petersburg, Major Giles B. Cooke noted in his diary that he met "Mr. Conneley, an English gentleman who came over to this country to see what could be seen."[10] Conolly must have made a stronger impression on Captain Frank Potts, of Longstreet's staff, who met him on the second of April just after learning of Lee's plan to evacuate Petersburg. In the confusion of those last hours before Richmond fell, Conolly's invitation to a dinner party on the eve of Confederate destruction formed a vivid part of Potts's recollections of the day.[11]

If his diary fairly represented his activities, Conolly spent much of his time with southern women, at least two of whom left written impressions of him. Malvina Black Gist, an attractive young war widow much given to the frenetic parties attended by soldiers in the capital, wrote approvingly of Conolly, "he seems to have plenty of money, and lives here in great style for war times."[12] Sara Rice Pryor, who grudgingly acceded to Lee's request that she provide a room for Conolly while he visited Petersburg, found to her surprise that "the M.P. proved a most agreeable guest, a fine-looking Irish gentleman with an irresistibly humorous, cheery fund of talk."[13]

For all these kind words, however, the reactions of his acquaintances suggest that some southerners were at a loss to explain his visit but were too polite to question him about it. The *Richmond Whig*,[14] calling Conolly "a genial and accomplished Irishman," went on to say that the "arrival of Mr. Conolly in the Confederate States, at this time, can hardly be deemed an event of any public significance." Although the newspaper predicted a cordial welcome for the M.P., it left the impression that it was very odd indeed he should have turned up just then.

Not without coincidence both Major General Wilcox and the Liverpool *Albion* used the same word, eccentric, to describe the traveler from Ireland. The quixotic nature of his visit—pressing on into danger after the pragmatic goal of blockade running had been thwarted—amply supports their opinion. Conolly's conduct before the fall of Richmond, though unremarkable in other circumstances, was rather frivolous given the time and place. He summed it up best himself with his comment about taking "a parting cup to our next merry meeting" as the flames engulfed the city. In both North and South, his attraction for women half his age and easy, alcohol-tinged companionship with shallow men like William Allen in Richmond and William

[10]Diary of Major Giles B. Cooke, 30 Mar. 1865, VHS.
[11]Potts, *Death of the Confederacy*, p. 7.
[12]Diary of Malvina Black Gist, quoted in Jones, ed., *Heroines of Dixie*, p. 380.
[13]Pryor, *My Day*, pp. 235–36.
[14]*Richmond Whig*, 6 Mar. 1865.

Angier in Philadelphia resonate with Conolly's style of life at home, though hardly to his credit.

Despite his eccentricities, his rakish indulgences, and his lack of vision in larger matters, however, on a personal level Conolly undoubtedly had winning ways. He was a charmer. His friends in Ireland and England as well as in Richmond affirmed repeatedly that Tom Conolly was for all his faults just too engaging for anyone to dislike. And students of southern history can be thankful too that he applied his obsession for notetaking in full measure throughout his months in America. A less adventuresome person than Conolly would have stayed at home. A less flamboyant one would have written a duller diary.

* * * *

After his return to Castletown, Conolly resumed his proprietary and parliamentary duties as before. He must still have been something of a celebrity during the general election held only two months after his voyage from America. He was unopposed then and again in the election three years later. His view of the world remained much the same, and he still professed to speak for "all those who were interested in authority, property, and religion in Ireland."[15] This perspective implied, among other things, a dread of what would follow if the Anglican church in Ireland were disestablished, as was proposed by Gladstone during the 1868 election campaign. Concerning this measure, "the Papists . . . will run their entire strength for G[ladstone]," wrote Conolly to Disraeli, "but we have measured them before and they will not prevail."[16] He was wrong. Although he survived the challenge as handsomely as before in his own constituency, his party and church did not. Even his district in rural Donegal did not remain a cozy, safe seat much longer. In the next election, in 1874, Conolly faced opposition and, as the less popular winner in a two-member district, came within an ace of being unseated.[17]

To villagers in Celbridge, which lies just outside the stone gates leading down an avenue of lime trees to Castletown House, it might have appeared that life at the great house had returned to routine in the summer of 1865. Certainly Tom Conolly's reputation for reckless living had not suffered from the voyage to America. Indeed, his adventure entered into local legend in garbled and almost folkloric form. In this version Conolly was said to have lost his ship in action with the Federal blockading fleet. After visiting the

[15]Account of Conolly's comments in the House, 11 Feb. 1866, *Hansard's Parliamentary Debates*, Vol. 181, col. 707.

[16]Thomas Conolly to Benjamin Disraeli, 26 Oct. 1868, Disraeli MSS, quoted in David Thornley, *Isaac Butt and Home Rule* (London, 1964), p. 34.

[17]*PERI*, pp. 102, 108, 116.

South, he then supposedly worked his way back across the Atlantic—not just the Chesapeake Bay—as an ordinary seaman. As the ship neared the Irish coast en route to England, so the story went, he jumped overboard and swam home, reaching Donegal in time to stand for reelection.

The consequences of living beyond his means could not be put off indefinitely, however. Conolly may have ignored the financial loss incurred in blockade running—in truth, that investment was but a small thing when set against the long-term strain on his income that his level of consumption represented—but even he could see that something had to be done. Belt-tightening measures were not enough. Only a year after returning from America, Conolly's brother Richard, a diplomat in Peking, congratulated him on solving the crisis at hand by doing the unthinkable—once again—by alienating patrimony: "Thank God a sale of a *portion* of the property will set you right. That infernal word '*sale*' [;] I hope & trust that from this [day] on it will be banished from our family vocabulary."[18]

Change came to Tom Conolly's personal life as well when he decided at last to marry and settle down. It was not a titled lady in London who caught his eye, however, but the pretty daughter of a local businessman. Sarah Eliza Shaw, like Nannie Thomas in Richmond and Lena Peters in Philadelphia, had hardly reached her majority when Conolly took an interest in her—at the time of their wedding in 1868 she was twenty-one to his forty-five. No doubt Conolly was captivated by her dowry as well as her beauty, for her father, Joseph Shaw, of Temple Mills House, Celbridge, reckoned that £10,000 was a fair enough price for installing a miller's daughter as mistress of the grandest country house in Ireland.

The infusion of cash from his father-in-law postponed Conolly's need to mend his ways, at least for the moment, especially when he had a young wife to show the attractions of London and the Continent. Shortly after their marriage, in fact, the Conollys became a familiar sight in the French capital, vying in good-natured competition with Tom's friend, Napoleon III, to see whose carriage was more splendidly turned out.[19] (Conolly won; his horses were shod in silver.) And, in a short time, the Conolly succession seemed assured with the birth of Thomas in 1870, Catherine in 1871, William in 1872, and Edward Michael in 1874.[20]

---

[18]Richard Conolly to Thomas Conolly, 10 Nov. 1866, Conolly MSS, quoted by permission of the Board of Trinity College Dublin.

[19]Boylan, "The Conollys of Castletown," p. 45.

[20]The first child, Thomas, lived only ten days. Those who survived infancy were another Thomas (1870–1900), Catherine (1871–1947), William (1872–1895), and Edward Michael (1874–1956). Catherine married the fifth baron Carew in 1904.

These portents—generous in-laws and a wealth of heirs—were unfortunately misleading signs for the family's future. The legendary Conolly inheritance was not proof against the consequences of long-term agricultural decline, which afflicted great landlords and tenant farmers alike across the Irish countryside.[21] Tom was beginning at last to address the imbalance between expenses and income, but, just as he began to do so, he died at the early age of fifty-three. Unlike some of the Confederate soldiers he had met in America, he did not die on the field. To him was given a quiet death, in his own bed at the ancestral home that had come down to him from Speaker Conolly. The end came on 10 August 1876 after some months of declining health, months that outside the walls of Castletown witnessed heated speculation in the constituency about who would succeed the Right Honorable Member for County Donegal.[22]

When Tom was buried in the family vault, over which stands a marble effigy of Speaker Conolly, his young widow and four small children faced debts accumulated from years of living beyond the family's means and a declining base of agricultural rents.[23] The next decades were indeed hard for the family, and not just financially. The second son, William, died at twenty-two, and the eldest, Thomas, at thirty. Tom Conolly's heir and namesake, like sons of the landed gentry throughout the United Kingdom, had followed the tradition of military service, in young Thomas's case leading to a captaincy in the Scots Greys. And like his uncle Arthur Wellesley Conolly, who fell in the Crimea, he died a soldier's death at an obscure South African crossroads in 1900. The other children lived longer. The third son, Edward Michael, lived at Castletown for many years, and then it was the son of the only daughter, Catherine, who inherited the estate.

In the 1960s, after a quarter of a millennium in Conolly hands, the house of Speaker Conolly was sold. To the benefit of the Irish nation and students

[21]The population of County Donegal had fallen 20 percent between 1831 and 1861, of County Kildare, 16 percent. With these declines the rents of the great landlords fell as well (*PERI*, pp. 267, 285). On the decline of the landed gentry in Ireland, see Mark Bence-Jones, *Twilight of the Ascendancy* (London, 1987).

[22]The London *Times* was strangely silent on Conolly's demise, with only two lines appearing in the death notices (12 Aug. 1876). Aspirants to Conolly's seat lost no time in declaring their candidacy. Indeed, much of the maneuvering had taken place before Conolly died. "It was anticipated a few months ago that Mr. Conolly would retire in consequence of the state of his health, and the names of several gentlemen were mentioned as prospective candidates" (14 Aug. 1876).

[23]Although buried at first in the Conolly family mortuary chapel attached to the ruins of St. Mochua's Church, Kildrought Parish, Conolly's remains were moved later to the new family plot his widow built next to the new Protestant church that stands just inside the gates of Castletown.

of fine architecture everywhere, it was later purchased by the Honorable Desmond Guinness for the Irish Georgian Society. The society now maintains its headquarters at Castletown, which once again receives visitors from around the world who still marvel, as the Ascendancy gentry did, at the house of Conolly.

* * * *

Evelyn Waugh has Lord Marchmain, in indolent, self-imposed Venetian exile, say, "I suppose it is a disgraceful thing to inherit great responsibilities and to be entirely indifferent to them. I am all the socialists would have me be, and a great stumbling-block to my own party."[24] Although Tom Conolly did not neglect his proprietary duties as a great landlord to the extent of absenteeism, he can be faulted for other shortcomings. Any assessment of his life would be incomplete, however, if it only considered his financial imprudence and admittedly reckless ways. As his many friends knew, Tom Conolly was a man of many traits, at the same time both amiable and eccentric, both charming and irresponsible.

Let then a kindlier voice have the last words. On learning of Conolly's death, Lady St. Helier wrote, "his hospitality was unbounded, and his house was always full. There were horses to ride, there were cars to be driven; there was an excellent cook and plenty of champagne. . . . Dear old Tom Conolly! He was the kindest, the brightest, the most delightful of people, perfect as a host, a kind and staunch friend and universally beloved."[25]

---

[24]Evelyn Waugh, *Brideshead Revisited: The Sacred and Profane Memories of Captain Charles Ryder* (Boston, 1945), p. 99.

[25]Quoted in Boylan, "The Conollys of Castletown," p. 45.

APPENDIX A

EDITORIAL METHOD

Thomas Conolly recorded his American diary in a large ledger, bound with a leather spine and marbled paper covers, on the title page of which he wrote, "Log of 1st. Expedition to America beginning 23rd. day of February 1865 being two days before my birth day Thomas Conolly." He made the last entry on 26 May 1865. The transcription presented in this book was made from a photocopy of the diary given to the Virginia Historical Society by Desmond Fitz-Gerald, a trustee of the Castletown Foundation, County Kildare, Ireland, which owns the original. Questionable passages in the photocopy were checked against the original during a research trip to Ireland in 1987.

Conolly created three other records during the voyage, which are also the property of the Castletown Foundation and which are cited in the notes to this book. These are referred to as the "rough diary," the "log book," and the "scrapbook." The rough diary contains intermittent entries from 26 November 1864 to 1 February 1865 and miscellaneous comments. The log book, a printed ledger for a ship's log, contains additional notations made during the voyages of the *Emily* and *Florence*. The scrapbook, a large, leather-bound ledger with ruled blue pages and "Day-Book" printed on the spine, was apparently purchased in Richmond, Virginia. It served Conolly as a file for newspaper clippings, letters, sheet music, receipts, and other scraps of paper accumulated during his trip. Other manuscripts of Thomas Conolly owned by the Castletown Foundation include his diaries for the years 1853, 1857, 1858, 1861, 1863, and 1864 and a European travel diary of 1870–71. Except for the 1870–71 account, these diaries include only brief notes, listings of guests at dinner parties, and short accounts of events attended but few extended passages of narrative.

The transcription of the diary presented in this volume employs no modernizations or silent corrections of grammar, spelling, punctuation, or capitalization. Some standardization of presentation is unavoidable, however, especially given Conolly's failure to maintain a regular format throughout and his tendency to scribble in the margins. There are seven general categories of deviations from a literal rendering of the original manuscript.

First, several types of notation in the original have been omitted. These include Conolly's original page numbers, running heads, and roman-numeral section divisions (which occurred largely but not invariably with the beginning of a new day's entry). Also omitted are Conolly's frequent marginal notations of the time of day when the event he was describing took place.

Second, the beginning of a new day's entry has been standardized. The date before each day's entry has been put in a regular form, and the following entry appears as a new paragraph.

Third, Conolly's superior letters have been brought down to the line. No contraction has been silently expanded, however.

Fourth, Conolly's numerous marginal references and references to notes at the back of the diary, have been incorporated into the footnotes of this book. A few, short cryptic references have been omitted.

Fifth, entries in Conolly's listing of appendixes, compiled at the back of the diary, are incorporated in the footnotes of this book at the points at which he referred to the appendix listings. (The appendixes themselves were scraps of paper, newspaper clippings, and receipts that he collected during his travels and placed in his scrapbook, not in the diary.)

Sixth, Conolly collected at the back of the diary numerous signatures of people he met, and in the footnotes to this book, the phrase "signature at back of diary" precedes the signature and text, if any, that Conolly added after the name.

Seventh, because Conolly's penmanship ranged from a mildly difficult but regular hand to an infuriating scrawl, whenever a likely transcription for a particularly inscrutable word or passage came to mind, it was enclosed in brackets with a question mark. When no guess was possible, the word or phrase was rendered as [*illegible*].

Footnotes appear at the first mention of every individual for whom identification could be made. Some of these naturally are less than firm identifications and have been noted as such. An attempt has been made to include references in these notes of identification to important passages elsewhere in the diary that involve the individuals mentioned. Of course, the reader should refer to the index for a comprehensive listing of entries for each individual. Because Conolly met many Confederate generals who are well known, most of the notes identifying these men are limited to life dates, ranks, and page references in Ezra J. Warner's *Generals in Gray*. The same treatment applies to the Union generals Conolly mentioned, with reference to Warner's companion volume, *Generals in Blue*. Notes identifying the more prominent people Conolly met are similarly limited, with references to standard printed sources, such as the *Dictionary of American Biography* and the *Biographical Directory of the Confederacy*.

APPENDIX B

25 February 1823	Born
1848	On death of his father, becomes master of Castletown
1849	Appointed to take his father's place in the House of Commons
30 July 1852	Wins first election
5 November 1853	Sister Louisa Augusta (Conolly) Langford drowns
5 November 1854	Younger brother Arthur Wellesley Conolly killed at Inkerman
8 April 1857	Returned in uncontested election
7 May 1859	Returned in uncontested election
26 November 1864	Sets out on American journey
26 February 1865	Reaches America
17 May 1865	Leaves America
21 July 1865	Returned in uncontested election
1 September 1868	Marries Sarah Eliza Shaw of Celbridge
24 November 1868	Returned in uncontested election
1 September 1870	Eldest son Thomas born
20 October 1871	Daughter Catherine born
29 October 1872	Son William born
10 February 1874	Narrowly wins contested election
22 February 1874	Son Edward Michael born
10 August 1876	Dies at Castletown

APPENDIX C

CHRONOLOGY OF CONOLLY'S AMERICAN TRAVELS

November 1864–May 1865

26 November 1864	Sets out from Summerhill, County Meath, for rendezvous with *Emily* at Cardiff
27 November	Reaches Waterford and takes passage to Cardiff
7 December	Departs from Cardiff on board *Emily*
16 December	Reaches Madeira
20 December	Naval inquest sends *Emily* to Spain for repairs
4 January 1865	Departs from Madeira on blockade runner *Florence*
13 January	Arrives at Bermuda
25 January	Departs from Bermuda on *Florence*
29 January	Arrives at Nassau
2 February	Departs from Nassau on *Florence*
3 February	*Florence* collides with another vessel
5 February	*Florence* returns to Nassau
23 February	Departs from Nassau on *Owl*
26 February	Arrives at Shallotte Inlet, N.C.
2 March	Arrives at Fayetteville, N.C.
5 March	Arrives at Raleigh, N.C.
8 March	Arrives at Richmond, Va., by train
13 March	Visits Jefferson Davis in Richmond
15 March	Travels to Petersburg, Va., to see R. E. Lee
17 March	Returns to Richmond
25 March	Visits fleet at Drewry's Bluff, Va.
25 March	Returns to Richmond
27 March	Visits Petersburg again
30 March	Visits Lee in the field

31 March	Returns to Richmond
3 April	Flees Richmond
6 April	Reaches Chatterton, King George Co., Va., on the Potomac River
8–9 April	Crosses Potomac River with T. N. Conrad
15 April	Arrives at Baltimore on schooner *Abeona*
15 April	Visits Washington, D.C.
16 April	Returns to Baltimore
17 April	Arrives at Philadelphia
21 April	First trip to New York City
22 April	Returns to Philadelphia
2 May	Second trip to New York City
8 May	Returns to Philadelphia
? May	Third trip to New York City
? May	Trip to Niagara Falls
? May	Returns to New York City
17 May	Leaves New York City on board *Scotia*
26 May	En route to Liverpool, the *Scotia* reaches the Irish coast and the diary ends

Appendix D

Almanac	E. B. Long with Barbara Long, *The Civil War Day by Day: An Almanac, 1861–1865* (Garden City, N.Y., 1971)
BDC	Jon L. Wakelyn, *Biographical Directory of the Confederacy*, Frank E. Vandiver, advisory editor (Westport, Conn., and London, 1977)
BRCC	Ezra J. Warner and W. Buck Yearns, *Biographical Register of the Confederate Congress* (Baton Rouge, 1975)
Blue	Ezra J. Warner, *Generals in Blue: Lives of the Union Commanders* (Baton Rouge, 1964)
CMH	Clement A. Evans, ed., *Confederate Military History*, 12 vols. (Atlanta, 1899)
CSO	Joseph H. Crute, Jr., *Confederate Staff Officers, 1861–1865* (Powhatan, Va., 1982)
CV	*Confederate Veteran*
DAB	*Dictionary of American Biography*
DNB	*Dictionary of National Biography*
ECW	Patricia Faust, ed., *Historical Times Illustrated Encyclopedia of the Civil War* (New York, 1986)
Gray	Ezra J. Warner, *Generals in Gray: Lives of the Confederate Commanders* (New Orleans, 1959)
LC	Robert K. Krick, *Lee's Colonels: A Biographical Register of the Field Officers of the Army of Northern Virginia* (Dayton, Ohio, 1979)
log book	Conolly's account of the voyages of the *Emily* and *Florence,* in the possession of the Castletown Foundation
MHM	*Maryland Historical Magazine*
NA	National Archives, Washington, D.C.

NCT   Weymouth T. Jordan, Jr., comp., with Louis H. Manarin,
            North Carolina Troops, 1861–1865: A Roster, 9 vols. to
            date (Raleigh, 1966–)
OB   Virginia Historical Society *Occasional Bulletin*
OR   U.S. War Department, *The War of the Rebellion: A
            Compilation of the Official Record of the Union and
            Confederate Armies* (128 vols.; Washington, D.C., 1880–
            1901)
ORN   U.S. Navy Department, *Official Records of the Union and
            Confederate Navies in the War of the Rebellion* (30 vols.;
            Washington, D.C., 1894–1927)
PERI   Brian M. Walker, ed., *Parliamentary Election Results in
            Ireland, 1801–1922* (Dublin, 1978).
rough diary Conolly's intermittent diary, from November 1864 to
            February 1865, in the possession of the Castletown
            Foundation
scrapbook   Conolly's ledger used to file letters, receipts, and other
            pieces of paper accumulated during his trip, in the
            possession of the Castletown Foundation
SHSP   J. William Jones et al., eds., *Southern Historical Society
            Papers* (52 vols. and 2 vol. index; Richmond, 1876–1959)
VHS   Virginia Historical Society

INDEX

143